Winning at Work
Without
Losing at Love

Other books authored or coauthored by Stephen Arterburn:

Addicted to "Love"
The Angry Man
Drug-Proof Your Kids
Faith that Hurts, Faith that Heals
Fifty-Two Simple Ways to Say "I Love You"
Gentle Eating
Growing Up Addicted
Hand-Me-Down Genes & Second-Hand Emotions
Hooked on Life
How Will I Tell My Mother?
The Life Recovery Bible (General Editor)
Twelve-Step Life Recovery Devotional
The War Is Over but Children Still Have Questions
When Love Is Not Enough
When Someone You Love Is Someone You Hate

Winning at Work Without Losing at Love

Stephen Arterburn

THOMAS NELSON PUBLISHERS
Nashville • Atlanta • London • Vancouver

To

Dorothy Grasty

the person who got me started in my career by giving me my first job in Fort Worth, Texas, as a nurse's aide two nights a week.

I have never met anyone who worked harder, won more, and did so with such warmth and love. She is a winner at work and at home with her husband, Donald, their kids, and their grandkids.

Thank you, Dorothy, for all you gave to me and to everyone who ever worked with you.

Published in Nashville, Tennessee, by Thomas Nelson, Inc., Publishers, and distributed in Canada by Word Communications, Ltd., Richmond, British Columbia.

The Bible version used in this publication is THE NEW KING JAMES VERSION. Copyright © 1979, 1980, 1982, 1990, Thomas Nelson, Inc., Publishers.

All names and events have been fictionalized for protection of privacy.

Excerpts from "Calling His Own Plays" by Barry Horn are reprinted with permission of THE DALLAS MORNING NEWS.

Arterburn, Stephen, 1953–
    Winning at work without losing at love / Stephen Arterburn.
      p.   cm.
    ISBN 0-8407-9703-6
    1. Success in business—United States. 2. Quality of life—United States. 3. Work and family—United States. 4. Self-actualization (Psychology) I. Title.
    HF5386.A765   1995
    650.1—dc20   94-33977
                                                          CIP

Printed in the United States of America.
      1 2 3 4 5 6 — 99 98 97 96 95 94

Contents

ACKNOWLEDGMENTS

Deep gratitude for the hard work of Lela Gilbert, Connie Neal, Lila Empson, and Esther Fitzpatrick for turning a rough manuscript into a complete book.

Thanks to Victor Oliver of Oliver Nelson Publishing for continuing to believe in me enough to continue to get my thoughts and ideas in print.

A special thanks to my wife, Sandy, who is my greatest motivator and has insured that I won at work and at love. Thanks, Sandy, for loving me even through the rough times.

Introduction

I have been amazed to discover that some of the gurus of success have achieved that success not from starting a business or from working their way from the bottom to the top of an organization but from selling tapes on success. One of the wealthiest seminar producers was a failure until he went to the library and found all the success principles from writers down through the ages, put them together into a seminar, and then made millions from the tape sales. One of the most prosperous real estate gurus didn't make his big money selling land; he made it from selling tapes on how to buy and sell property. Now I give these people a lot of credit for what they did do, but if following their advice leaves the followers a little empty, it might be due to the lack of personal experience that forms the foundation of the material.

I want you to know the foundation of the principles in this book that you have decided to dedicate some of your valuable time to reading. I want you to know that these principles came from the experience of starting at the bottom, working hard, being blessed by God, and using the most valuable tool of winners—perseverance. As of this writing, I have never made a dollar from selling a success tape (but the other guys have done so well at it, I am going to look into how you do that). I wasn't born with a silver spoon or fork in my mouth. I have been fortunate to have accomplished much, but I look with regret on what I could have done if I had been more focused on priorities much earlier in my life. I don't take credit for all I have done because the tools to do it came from

INTRODUCTION

my Creator and a family heritage of hardworking winners. I hope to pass on to others what was passed down to me.

One of my prize possessions is a picture of my grandmother, known as Mother Art, working at her first full-time job. She was about age six at the time of the photo, working at her father's sugarcane mill. They grew the cane and then they harvested it and brought it to the mill. The mill consisted of a huge crushing rock that was rotated over its base by a donkey. The donkey walked around and around as the workers, including my grandmother, pushed the cane under the stone to be crushed. The sweet juice was boiled until it became molasses that they sold to make a living.

My great-grandfather not only knew how to make molasses and provide for his family; he knew how to create a family full of love and character. I am grateful that somehow he knew how to grow people as well as a business because he passed on to me a grandmother I admire more than any other woman alive. Today, at age ninety-two, she lives alone, independent but connected to a huge host of friends and family who love her and honor her. She is a winner, and I am thrilled to be carrying her genes in all my endeavors. Her life has been fulfilled through working hard, serving others, and making a contribution.

My grandmother married a man who, like her father, ran his own business and succeeded at most of whatever he did. Although he was not wealthy, he was able to afford three houses. He and my grandmother lived in one. He rented one to my dad for a while, and we lived there until I was five. The third was a house on Lake Leon. The lake house provided him and all of us with countless hours of fun fishing, swimming, and waterskiing.

We called my grandfather Dad Art, and I was his namesake, taking his middle name, Forrest, as mine. That name got me a $100 U.S. savings bond from him each year on my birthday along with a sense of being favored. This huge, tough

Texan gave me the feeling that I could do anything; I could accomplish whatever I wanted. There was no problem he could not figure out. He loved his family and served his community, showing me and all the other grandkids what it meant to be a winner at work and at love.

Dad Art earned his living by making tools that would fish broken drill bits out of oil wells back in the Texas oil boom of the 1940s. He was a man who could find a way to do just about everything on his own. He and his sons built their own house on the lake. The ceiling ended up about two feet lower than most ceilings, but they rationalized that the less headroom, the cheaper it would be to heat in winter. That seemed to be more important than the fact that people over five four would get hit in the nose by a light fixture if they didn't watch where they were going. Though no home construction genius, my grandfather thought if someone else could build something, he could, too. I remember our first trip to the Houston Astrodome. He pulled out his tape measure to write down just how big those metal beams were. One never knew when that kind of information would come in handy.

One of the myths of manhood, real men don't cry, was never one that my grandfather had a problem with. His machine shop was on the same property as his house, so every day he went home for lunch. After a quick lunch, he went to his bedroom, stretched out on the bed, and watched "As the World Turns" and "Search for Tomorrow" on the first color television set in our town. My memory is quite clear on its installation and the fact that you had to use a magnetic wand to get the best color from the set. My memory is also quite clear of that huge man who could do anything, lying there, crying through those soap operas. He was not ashamed, either. Those were his people, and he loved them like his own family. Sometimes I think his tears might have been for joy since no matter how many problems our family had, they weren't nearly as bad as the entangled messes thought up by the scriptwriters of the soaps.

Dad Art had five boys. Every one has been a hardworking contributor to the American economy. They haven't accepted handouts; they have all paid their own way. They worked together and played together, forming an almost complete softball team. Some of my uncles were better at business and others were better at creating a home, but they all were examples that you can win at providing for your family if you persist against the odds.

My dad was a winner who carried on the entrepreneurial tradition of his father. He created and owned and operated businesses all his life. He had fast-food restaurants. He owned coin-operated Laundromats. He was always looking for another way to earn extra money. Even his failed venture into owning Pepe's Peanut machines was a way for him to find additional money for three boys who needed a college education. Through all of his ventures, material wealth and huge capital gains eluded my father, but he never gave up looking for another way to turn time and effort into money.

My mother was a hard worker who sacrificed a life of teas and coffees for a life of hard work. She owned and operated beauty salons. She probably would have become a wealthy beauty salon magnate had she not discovered that she possessed the one thing a beauty salon owner cannot have— an allergy to hair spray. Even with the allergy she continued to operate her salons until "the boys" were assured of being able to go to college.

This family work ethic of my great-grandparents, grandparents, and parents was modeled for me by my two brothers, one three years older and the other six years older than me. Before they were ten, they were delivering newspapers early in the morning on a motor scooter, which they rode up until the day we moved out of Ranger to Bryan, Texas, where law enforcement officials were much less tolerant of children operating fast and heavy machinery. In those early days I watched them work, and I watched them spend their own money. It had an impact. It laid an internal foundation of belief in the value of work and the joy of creating money. I never thought of getting something for nothing.

It wasn't just money that I wanted to go after. I had enough powerful influences to help me see that earning money for yourself was different from making a contribution and a difference in this world. My grandfather single-handedly worked to have a water tower put in at the lake so all who lived there could have fresh drinking water rather than have to bring it from town. My father did more for his church than just about anyone in our town. I remember going with my father to deliver food to families who lived in one-room houses whose only source of light hung from a single cord in the middle of the room. My mother's mother was always taking care of someone or cooking one of her otherworldly German chocolate cakes to give away. On a meager sum of Social Security money she always found a way to give back and give away. I learned from all of this the balance between working hard, making money, and making your mark on the world.

My first job earned me minimum wage for working in the cotton fields of Texas A&M University. To produce hybrid plants, my coworkers and I had to seal shut the cotton blossoms so no bee could rob the pollen and give it to another plant. I spent every sun-drenched backbreaking day of my summer bending over cotton plants and gluing their flower petals together. Many nights we irrigated the fields, sometimes putting in eighty hours of work in a week. We weren't just earning money. We were assisting in the development of a strain of cotton whose plants would be void of a toxic pit found in all cotton plants. The work we did enabled cotton seeds to be shipped to developing countries where they grew the plants to produce fibers for clothing and they used the excess seeds to make flour or ate the seeds whole. In our own small way we had been a part of doing something important for the world while earning minimum wage.

I can still remember the elation of getting my own paycheck and being able to spend it any way I wanted. (Sadly, I would not learn the art of saving money until much later on.) With that first paycheck I became a proud part of the U.S. workforce. Those of us within this workforce, by our individual efforts, are making our country strong by making it more productive as we find ways to improve our productivity. I write this book for fellow workers, and I encourage you to see the great value in what you do, even if the financial rewards are less than you would like.

Alongside my family of workers, I was surrounded by plenty of losers outside the family. I saw people in our town who refused to work and had the idea that they were entitled to everything everyone else had, even though they were unwilling to put in the work and risk the failure. I watched a well-respected pastor fall in love with a wealthy widow, tear up his family, and destroy the faith of hundreds who were shattered by his example as a loser. I have seen top managers of companies who thought nothing of sleeping with anyone and everyone available. I have watched them drag home sexually transmitted diseases to their wives and, upon diagnosis, beg for forgiveness and a chance to live their lives over. All of the losers made just as big an impression on me as the winners. They all helped me decide early on that I would do what I could to make a contribution but that effort would never take precedence over my family and home life.

My journey to where I am today began in college. I had so many problems there that people started coming to me for advice with theirs, and I felt destined to become a counselor. I pursued counseling in graduate school, but I found I wasn't very good at it for two reasons. The first was my impatience. I couldn't stand to sit and watch two people who had been lying to each other now lie to me in a marriage counseling session. I pushed the people too hard to get beyond the problem they had presented and to the real problem that they were too embarrassed or afraid to discuss. My supervisors, observing behind two-way mirrors, said I was too confrontational, too controlling. The other problem was that the world was too big and those counseling rooms too small. With every session I was more and more determined to be somewhere else than behind a closed door. My heart continued to want to help, but my talent just wasn't there.

While going to graduate school, I worked in a psychiatric hospital on the night shift as a nurse's aide. There, confronted with real problems and honest and desperate people, I found a new love that I have never left. Since that first night on the psych ward, I have always done something with psychiatric or addiction problems. I have not been confused about where my talents and interests are best used. I worked my way up the ladder of that little hospital until I was the program director there. The hospital was doing poorly, and I finally convinced the administrators to allow me to market it. They did, and it became filled with patients. The small twenty-six-bed facility eventually added over one hundred beds and gave me my first taste of success.

The company that owned the hospital moved me from Texas to California. I was transferred to the company's largest alcohol treatment facility that was only 50 percent occupied. I went there with a new administrator, and between the two of us, we had a waiting list for the place within six months. Next, I was moved to head a marketing division for the company, and then, I ran one-third of the hospitals and programs across the country. My one-third, thanks to three great managers under my supervision, made over one-half of the profit for the company. I had moved from a night shift orderly to a senior vice president in less than nine years. I knew marketing. I loved to see people who had not won before turn their careers around into a series of successes. As I moved up, others moved up. And as a result of all of us moving up, people who needed help were getting it.

My next move was both dumb and brilliant. Another company hired me away at double my salary and gave me thousands of shares of stock. But I didn't do my homework. I very quickly went from executive vice president to chairman of the board when the board fired my boss for mismanagement. When I took over this $250 million health-care company, what I thought was $80 million in receivables was actually $8 million. We were losing so much money that there was no way for the company to survive. The former management team had raised millions of dollars from junk bonds and used the money to pay millions of dollars for small hospitals that were worth nothing. In fact, many of them are boarded up today. I had a trustee appointed, and I put the company in Chapter 11. It was not much fun being chairman of a company going bankrupt, but the things I learned put me light-years ahead in experience. The worst thing that happened to my career turned out to be the best thing. I was down and depressed but determined not to make one little misstep destroy me.

In 1988, an extremely successful man named Dave Steffy committed to me that if I ever had an idea for a company that he liked, he would find the money for it. My idea was for a psychiatric health-care company named New Life Treatment Centers. Dave liked the idea, as did his friend Dick Ragsdale. Together they found the few millions of dollars it took to fund my idea. I am greatly indebted to them and the others they convinced that it would be a good investment. All of us working together in a very tough industry took the company from zero to $40 million in revenues in five years while many others in our industry went out of business or were plagued by scandal. In 1993, I was awarded an Entrepreneur of the Year Award by *Inc. Magazine* and Merrill Lynch.

In addition to what I was doing in business I had become

a published writer and public speaker. I have published sixteen books, this being the seventeenth, with my name on them. They have been translated into six other languages. Seven have made it onto best-seller lists. I also published another fourteen books that don't have my name on them. (Please believe me when I say I'm not bragging. I'm just trying to convince you I didn't get the stuff in this book out of the library.) Three years ago I was awarded two honorary doctorate degrees.

Although I abandoned counseling in small rooms, I am finally back to where I started, only the room is larger. Each day I cohost a radio program called the "Minirth Meier New Life Clinic." It is heard each day by over one million people. Some of them call and explain their problems, and rather than expect me to merely listen, they expect me to tell them what to do, the very thing my supervisors in graduate school criticized me for. It is the most fun and rewarding thing that I do. It is just another example of never giving up when you are told you are inadequate in a certain area. You never know when that inadequacy will be used to further your success.

While I was doing all of this, my wife and I started a swimwear company that she ran for seven years until we sold it twice when our daughter came along. We sold it once to a man who went to prison for a check-kiting scheme. Fortunately, his check to us was good, but we got the company back and sold it again. Sandy also ran her own advertising agency. Now she has a small company that sells rubber stamps, and it will probably make more money than anything I have ever done. All of this time, we kept our marriage and our faith intact, and we raised one of the most incredible human beings ever born, Madeline.

Both Sandy and I know that love and life must come alongside making a living. You don't have to sacrifice one for the other. It would be foolish to do so. We are people who persevere, stay focused, and allow God to use us to make a contribution. We are not the ultimate successes in terms of the world's standards, but we have found fulfillment. That, dear reader, is what I hope you are seeking in reading this book, and I hope you find how to get it. Thanks for allowing me to share a bit of my journey. Turn the page to discover that you really can win at work without losing at love.

Part 1

Balancing the Mission, the Money, and the Meaning of Your Life

CHAPTER ONE

The Great Balancing Act

You can tell from the title, this book is about being successful in all areas of life. To find that kind of balanced success, you must have a life mission, handle money well, and discover the meaning of your life. If one of them gets out of kilter, your personal life and career may begin to self-destruct. At the same time, when one of them is ignored, imbalance occurs. The goal of this book is to help you consider, develop, and balance these three areas of life to your advantage. When you balance them you will be winning at work without losing at love.

This book is about developing a whole and fulfilling life. I am talking about how to make money and enjoy it once you make it rather than watch it destroy you and your family. This book is about how to win in all aspects of life so that others win right alongside you. If you want to live with purpose and have meaningful relationships, this book will help you find what you are looking for. If you want to be considered successful, on the job and away from work, this book is for you.

By the time you finish reading, my goal for you is to be on your way toward achieving what you want to achieve. But I have a deeper concern in mind. My hope for you is that once you've found the success you desire, it will mean something to you. Let's make sure that when the payoff comes along, your friends and loved ones will still be around to celebrate your victory with you. Trophies lose their glow quickly without the applause of family and friends.

Success is a difficult word to define, and we'll take a closer look at what it means in the following pages. But let's make one thing clear at the outset:

Success is not something you achieve; success is something you become.

Winning in one endeavor does not make anyone successful. In fact, it often turns some into big-time losers in other parts of their lives. Newspapers and Hollywood tabloids are full of stories of sports and entertainment celebrities who got it all only to lose it all through drugs, suicide, or criminal involvement.

We can make the numbers work and make our way to the top of our chosen professions, but if we lose our souls, our families, and our freedom in the process, we are not successful in the broader sense of the word. If we lose ourselves in the process of becoming what we always wanted to be, we are headed into an abyss occupied by has-beens. The potential for a whole and satisfying life is never reached; true fulfillment is never attained.

We've all watched individuals who seem to have it all in terms of how the world views success; then they end up losing it all in the end. They are discussed sadly over dinner. We shake our heads, all the while thinking, *There but for the grace of God go I.* Clearly, winning in your career or finances is not the key to true success. Sometimes, it increases the height of the limb you're precariously perched on—until you pull out your very own self-destructive saw and saw it off.

For people who yearn for success, winning seems like the greatest possible experience. Living at the top seems like the geographical location they were destined to inhabit—at least until they look around and discover there is no one up there with them. "Lonely at the top" takes on new meaning when they experience the loneliness. As the adrenaline seeps out of the system, many winners wonder why they bothered to win. And yet they turn right around and start over again, setting out on an all-new, solitary search for another big win. They think, *Maybe if this one is bigger than the last, it will fix the hole in the stomach. Maybe it will fill the depressing emptiness that was enlarged rather than shrunk by that last success.*

If the foundation is not exactly right, no win at the top will be able to fill the cracks at the bottom. The wise person rebuilds the foundation before setting out to place the burden of more success on a weak one. It is also the wise person who discovers that the emptiness grows with each new achievement. It is contentment, not achievement, that lessens the pain of a winner (who knows he is losing out on some important aspects of life). Hope comes when the person learns to win in a way that increases her level of fulfillment rather than makes her realize how empty she is.

The Great Balancing Act

WOUNDS WOUNDING THE WOUNDED

The past decades have brought to public attention numerous lives of those who looked as if they had it all until their losses became a matter of public scorn or pity. Whether it was O. J. Simpson, Woody Allen, Ivan Boesky, Michael Milken, Jimmy Swaggart, Leona Helmsley, or Gary Hart, no one wounds the wounded like the wounded themselves.

I began writing this piece on Wednesday, April 27, 1994. That day our government shut down, observing a day of mourning for former President Richard Nixon, who died the previous week. What an example of perseverance and comeback ability! And what an example of the wounded wounding himself! There is no better example of a man who had it all—power, prestige, position, popularity—but threw it all away. At the height of his career, he wounded himself like no one else could have. I wonder what were the wounds of Richard Nixon? What was it in his life that led him to the top and then pulled him down so tragically? Thousands who never made headlines have lived out similar stories of grand achievement and then self-destruction. Wounded winners either lose all their winnings or can't enjoy what they have won.

Most successful people don't just suddenly win the big lottery. They often spend a lifetime overcoming some deficit, some woundedness, from their early years. These people fuel their success with the pain of the past. Work and the drive to be noticed and get ahead are attempts to medicate wounds. We see this pattern often, but we also see that in their attempts to medicate their wounds, they wound themselves further. Bear this in mind about all those who fail to find healing for their wounds: *they are bound to repeat what they fail to resolve.* If that statement disturbs you because it taps into some truth you know about yourself, you can act now to free yourself from what will thrust you in a downward spiral to loss.

WINNING AT WORK

All the well-known individuals we've watched crash and burn lost something important along the way to winning: they lost their love for other people. Some of them thought nothing of taking a hard-earned buck from someone else as long as it turned up in their own pockets. Others were more concerned with their own lusts and passions than with the people who had put their trust in them and stuck by them—even after the truth of their dark sides was revealed.

Those who fall from the top seem to love their successes more than they love other people, and eventually, they lose their balance and fall into a heap of embarrassment and humiliation for themselves, their families, and their friends. These men and women (and there are tens of thousands of them in our society) become obsessed with their success, but they still see themselves as victims. In their self-pity, they fail to see the pain they will someday inflict on others.

When well-known people fall victim to their own ambition, once the truth about them is known, their affluence can never pay enough to have their positions fully reinstalled in the hearts of those they hurt. They may have won once, but they've lost forever. Their tragic lives are a gift to all of us who want something better. They should inspire us to accomplish more than helping others by becoming a bad example *not* to follow.

THE SEARCH FOR 25 PERCENT MORE

Psychology Today (September–October 1992) published an article on ambition stating that the more successful people become, the more work oriented they get. There is something addictive about achievement, and that addicted-to-success attitude leads men and women to sacrifice family and friends to get more out of work. Less successful businesspersons are more likely to find satisfaction in areas outside work.

The Great Balancing Act

The sad reality for success-driven workers is that enough is never enough. No matter how much we achieve, no matter what level we attain, we always want 25 percent more. Wealth seems to enlarge the appetite for riches rather than satisfy it. Even those of us who have not had the business success of Donald Trump can understand his desire to buy and acquire more and more, looking for 25 percent more to bring satisfaction.

Most of us have thought that if we could find 25 percent more to add to our income, we would be satisfied, and the bills would all get paid on time. We feel so close to financial security, but we need a bit more to make it. Then at some future time, we look back and realize that while the 25 percent did come our way, our cost of living went up with the level of our income. We become like a cat chasing its tail, never able to quite catch it, never able to feel satisfied from getting it, but determined to continue the chase. The drive to acquire more is not calmed with acquisition; it is resolved when the focus turns to "being" more rather than "getting" more. Only then are we able to find true satisfaction from what we get.

It is not unusual to see a person experience failure and then respond to that failure with relief rather than remorse. Some people are more than happy to relax into a life of lowered ambition, and you can learn from them, too. There is a better and different way from failing and then no longer using your talent to the fullest. There is a way to keep ambition and yet relax with it, to enjoy seeking after success, and to actually find that ever-elusive satisfaction when you do. It can be done. It requires effort and planning and the understanding that money alone will not provide the satisfaction you long for.

WINNING AT WORK

MONEY AND MISERY

I live in a very affluent area of the nation: Orange County, California. I joke about it as the only place where kids on a scavenger hunt will ask you for a wide-screen TV! I grew up playing patty-cake, but around here it is more likely to be paté-cake. Millions of people look at this part of the world as the American dream being acted out in living color with no problem too big for anyone to handle. I know better.

Many of my affluent neighbors are not happy people. They are beset by divorces, by children in deep trouble, and by careers that never seem to provide them with enough of what they think they need. They drink a lot, they have affairs, and they abuse each other. Dissatisfaction reigns supreme.

I believe everything that plagues the rest of the nation seems to start here. If you wonder why there is a values vacuum in your community, and why kids don't know right from wrong, please wonder no more. The hole in our nation's soul started right here. The meaningless lives of people who have had multiple marriages, have abused drugs and alcohol, and have seen their children rebel in destructive ways point to the futility of living life for the sake of riches without the richness of underpinnings to traditional and moral values. It affects the careers and the personal lives of the rich and famous I know.

Midlife career change is a big indicator of personal dissatisfaction. In our dot on the map, people give their lives to learn a profession, only to abandon it in less time than it took to be trained. Doctors become real estate developers. Lawyers do only commercials for their law firms; they refuse to practice law because they hate it. I think the saddest of all are the psychologists. Apparently, no one told them that their lives would be spent in small rooms listening to people in pain. It seems as if some of them are looking only for good case histories to go in that next book. Once they hit the best-seller list, there will be no more need to see patients. Some therapists are in such pain that they can no longer handle the pain of clients. What once was a lifelong dream is now a shallow, monotonous nightmare.

Let me continue to nag a minute about professional psychologists. These people are supposed to be helping others make responsible changes and decisions in their lives. One of the most common problems I have seen among these Ph.D.'s is tax problems. The only way you can get a tax problem is to spend money you weren't supposed to spend rather than give it to the federal government. This dilemma is destroying their lives because they have such a hard time making back the money they threw away that should have gone to Uncle Sam in the first place. Giving unto Caesar what is Caesar's somehow becomes optional to them until an IRS letter states that the loan is over. In their misery they overspend and underdeduct, placing them in a financial vise that furthers their belief that they must abandon what they have spent a lifetime learning how to do. Their early successes and excess expectations of what they were entitled to end up destroying what could have been a wonderful career of helping people change.

Whatever the profession, however great the possibility of fame and fortune, emptiness inevitably occurs when there is an imbalance of priorities and a lack of a solid foundation. Without them, there is always confusion among the three basic elements that make up a career. Throughout this book, I'll refer to the three elements of every field of work: the *mission* you are on, the *money* you make from it, and the *meaning* that comes out of your endeavor or the meaning that comes from spending the money you make accomplishing the mission.

WINNING FEVER

Since I am originally from Texas, I grew up watching the Dallas Cowboys win. Tom Landry was an idol. He was a winner, and there are evidences in his personal life that he knew how to win off the field as well as on. America's team was my team, and I admired Tom Landry for his ability to maintain integrity and attract some stars, like Roger Staubach, who also lived out lives of integrity. Even when Landry started to lose on the field, he continued to win off the field. There were no scandals. No friends turned traitor to reveal a dark side of Landry unknown to the public. When I moved to California, I carried with me my love for the Dallas Cowboys.

After years of winning, the team started to perform poorly. It was purchased by a new owner, who brought in a new coach. After a few predictable rough spots, the team turned around and began to win. Like Tom Landry, this coach knew how to win on the field. I was excited. I loved watching them win again, and I was amazed at how one man so right for the times could make such a big difference in a team's performance. How did he do it? I found the truth about Jimmy Johnson in a *Dallas Morning News* article printed Sunday, September 6, 1992. It turned out to be a classic example of a man who wins at his work but loses at love.

One of Johnson's sons was asked about Jimmy's hobby of keeping fish in seven saltwater tanks. The boy explained, "The fish—they may be the perfect things for him to have around the house. If he had a dog or a cat they might bug him and expect something from him in return. The fish—they don't want to know him. They leave him alone."

Jimmy Johnson was quoted as saying, "I can't let people really know me. I don't want people to ever know me well enough to predict what I will do. That way I always remain in control." He went on to explain that he has never enjoyed a Thanksgiving meal with his family, has never celebrated Christmas, and has never exchanged gifts with his family. He said, "I don't remember when I stopped paying attention to those things."

The Great Balancing Act

Of his divorce, Jimmy Johnson said he had no reason to want to be married in Dallas where the job description was different from that of college football and his time would be devoted totally to the business of football. College coaches need wives. NFL coaches don't. He commented, "There are a lot of social functions to deal with in being a college football coach, and I don't have them anymore. There is fund raising and recruiting. You have relationships with a lot of people. In my opinion it was good I was married there."

The article ended with a final quote: "Just understand one thing. The only way I could have gotten to this point in my life is to have lived it the way I did. And that, like everything, comes with a price."

Winning always comes with a price, but when that price is every relationship you have, the price is too great. If you have to give up your family, you essentially are deciding that you are subhuman, a distinct breed, and the track you take will leave you feeling less of a person than when you achieved your first win. When the path toward winning is strewn with broken commitments and broken relationships because they didn't help you get where you wanted to go, you obviously were headed in the wrong direction.

What was predominant in Jimmy Johnson's career? He obviously understood his mission, and he knew the money it would bring if he achieved it. But he didn't seem to understand that sometimes a focus on the mission and the money robs people of meaning and the memories that would have meant more than any single win. That mistake is made by too many too late. Jimmy Johnson eventually lost his opportunity to coach the Cowboys. He still has time to discover that winning alone is not really winning at all.

WINNING AT WORK

LEARNING MISTAKES RATHER THAN LEARNING FROM THEM

The night I had the great honor of winning the Entrepreneur of the Year Award, also called the Socially Responsible Entrepreneur Award, presented by *Inc. Magazine,* Merrill Lynch, and Ernst and Young, was one I will never forget. It was a thrill to accept it while my wife and my wonderful team cheered me on. They were the ones who had made it possible for me to win, and although their names didn't make it onto the award, I knew the truth, and so did they! I was the first to receive an award, so after the applause and adrenaline faded, I settled back to listen to the other recipients' acceptance speeches.

One of the men had been accompanied to the awards event by his family. When the presenter announced his name, there was a ripple of polite applause, and that's all. No one cheered. No one jumped up and hugged him. There was no question that he, and he alone, had won the award. His speech was not an acceptance speech but a public apology to his wife and kids. He confessed that he had worked all his life to achieve, and now he regretted the dinners he'd missed and the championship games his sons had attended without him. He looked at the award and said, "But now it has all come down to this." His words sounded as empty as he looked. He put all his effort in one direction—succeeding—and in the end, satisfaction was nowhere to be found.

Mission, meaning, or money—what was missing in that man's world? What was too important? If we don't learn from others' mistakes, we learn to make their mistakes. It is in our best interest that we take notice of all those who have lost their lives making work their lives. My grandfather put it better than most when he said, "If the horse is dead, get off." We would rather spend our lives beating a dead horse because although we get nowhere doing it, we are not required to move out of our comfort zone. My challenge to you, the reader, is to examine your life. If you find the more you have, the less you feel like a human being, or if you are losing touch with the core of your being, it is time to get off that dead horse and onto something that will bring you life and fulfillment along with success.

LOSING AT WORK AND LOSING AT LOVE

All these examples are obviously of people too caught up in the mission or the money. Yet some people tip the scales too far in the direction of meaning. You may not be able to relate to the person who wins so much he or she feels like a loser. You may feel empty because you have never found a way to win.

When my wife and I were dating, we met a man I'll call Don. The bright, quick-witted fellow was in his fifteenth year of graduate school. He was studying to become a therapist, and that usually took two or three extra years after college graduation. Much to the amazement of his friends (and especially his in-laws!), he finally got a degree. Several years later we caught up with Don, only to learn that he hadn't worked in two years. All of that preparation time had amounted to nothing. The prolonged preparation was just an excuse not to perform.

If you met the guy, you would probably love him. He's great in conversation, and I've never seen a more caring father. All that is terrific, but it is overshadowed by the friction between Don and his wife. She wants a responsible partner who would at least attempt to hold down a job for more than six months. He sees himself as a victim of circumstances with every intention of working just as soon as "the right job" comes along.

Don is just as unbalanced as Jimmy Johnson and the award recipient. He isn't serving money, and he isn't serving a mission (except to avoid responsibility). He seems to be absorbed with the meaning of life and enjoying life—and consequently taking life as easy as possible. Don won't hold down a job because he is unwilling to face the reality that work is part of life. Johnson and the other man won't hold down a life outside the job. Both extremes are symptoms of the same problem, hooking hopes and dreams on only one dimension of life and failing to succeed at the great balancing act that leads to fulfillment.

Of course, there are many cases where a husband and a wife have chosen to reverse traditional roles—he has cared for the kids while she has become the primary breadwinner. This kind of arrangement can work if both understand the circumstances and agree with the need to make the necessary adjustments.

Don is another story. His self-destructive laziness causes tremendous frustration and disappointment for his wife. He doesn't know how to win at work; he doesn't even know how to stay in a job long enough to attempt to win. Don's pattern may have been in place for the past thirty years, but I haven't given up on him. I believe with a little help, there's still hope for him to change.

Don has been wounded somewhere along the way, and his wound has driven him to an imbalanced approach to life. Despite his self-destructive behavior, I still have hope for him. I know that healing from past wounds is possible, and that along with the healing can come a change in perspective and behavior. I know because I've seen those changes in myself.

GROWING UP ''DISADVANTAGED''

You may have found my words about others a bit harsh or critical. Allow me now to point that critical finger in my

The Great Balancing Act

direction. In my childhood, I enjoyed things that 99 percent of the people living in developing countries would die to have. We always had clean clothes and plenty to eat. By the standards of many people living around the globe, we might have been considered affluent. Well, we weren't affluent, but we weren't poor, either. In hindsight, I can see that the problem was never with what we had or what we didn't have. My problems began with the way I perceived my family's financial status.

As I entered the sixth grade, I came to the conclusion that I was a second-class person from a second-class family, inferior to all my friends. Being the youngest in our family, I was an ideal candidate for having feelings of inferiority. The baby of the family is allowed to do fewer things, and the phrase "too young" or "too small" becomes ingrained in the brain. It doesn't take long to realize that if you had not been born, the family would have existed just fine without you. To make matters worse, I got the distinct impression that at times my family wished I had not come along at all.

This foundation of feeling left out and being somewhat of an afterthought was laid in my early years. But the walls started going up in the sixth grade. During that watershed school year, a man in town invited all of the kids to participate in a Thursday afternoon dance class. The class was called a cotillion, and it was expected to transform self-centered sixth graders into civilized little patrons of the arts. I learned that all of my friends would be involved. In great excitement, I rushed home with the invitation.

It didn't take the parental wet blanket long to smother my hopes. My mom and dad informed me in no uncertain terms that the last thing we could afford was dance lessons. As I thought about my friends enjoying themselves without me, those old, familiar feelings of being left out and deprived rose up inside me like a bitter tide. This might seem like a very superficial wound to you, but I infected it with resentment and turned it into a deep, unhealed gash.

My friends couldn't understand why I wouldn't be spending Thursday afternoons with them. When they asked why, I became very creative. I never told them we were too poor to pay. Instead, I informed them rather piously that we didn't believe in dancing and that I didn't like dancing. Besides, if I ever needed them, I would have private lessons. This response seemed to satisfy their curiosity, but as they rode off with their parents to learn their social lessons, I walked home alone. Thursdays were lonely days for a little boy who felt second class.

Fridays were no better. Every Friday's conversation was the same. There were wiggles and squeals as my classmates relived embarrassing moments from the afternoon before. Dance steps that I would never know were rehearsed, and as I watched, it seemed to me that each child had something I lacked. I was an outsider, and there was nothing I could do to change it.

BORN TO LOSE?

Then came summer vacation. My friends happily drove off to Branson, Missouri, to summer camp. Wayne Newton and the other performers were not yet on the scene, but Camps Kanakuk and Kanacomo were. The boys I knew went to one camp, and the girls to the other. Of course, my parents couldn't afford to send me along.

Among the girls heading for Branson was Biddie Pratt—I was as deeply in love with her as you can be in the sixth grade. The night before Biddie left for camp, I soaked my bed with tears. My depression was so great that my mother finally loaded me into the car and drove me to Biddie's home. There I presented her with a tear-stained sacrifice of my love—my picture. I could never have humiliated myself more in the name of love than by offering that photograph to her.

The time of Biddie's absence dragged by, and there were rumors that she had danced with and kissed one of my friends. My wound deepened. My feelings of inferiority ripped at me. If only I had been a person of privilege, I could have been there to prevent that embrace. My family's lack of money had cost me my first love!

I was further humiliated by the fact that my parents didn't have a membership to Briarcrest Country Club. Briarcrest was a meager country club, more country than club. It was indeed in the midst of many briars, on the crest of a hillette. My friends would ask girls to meet them there to swim or to go to one of their dances. I couldn't go. As I saw it, I was locked out because I was a nobody.

There is nothing intrinsically wrong with being considered a nobody by a particular social class. In fact, there are many things very wonderfully right about it if you have the self-confidence to resist their view of you. But if the rejection of the "in" group becomes a part of your woundedness, it can be quite destructive.

For me, the sixth grade became a line of demarcation. It was a time when determination and drive began to flow through my veins. I was resolved to never be locked out or left behind again. I'd never feel second class again. The wounds of that lonely boy became the fuel that led to success in adult life. I couldn't become a workaholic at age twelve, but I began to adapt in other ways.

RISING ABOVE THE REST

I began to use every aptitude, every unique quality, and every talent I possessed to rise above the crowd. I learned to sing solos, fighting my stage fright to get the attention I loved. I became student director of the choir. I was a starting full-back, with letters in football and music. Perhaps more important than anything else, I learned how to be funny. I could turn anything into a joke. My pain forced me to develop a quick wit that got me through the tough times then and brought me better times of success later. You may not detect it from the words I write here, but I have been told by many people that I am the funniest person they have met. I am proud of that title, but it is one born out of much pain.

All along the way I acted in a manner that would elevate me above the mundane existence of a typical hometown boy. Texas A&M was almost in my backyard, and it was certainly good enough for my two brothers. But I insisted on going away to college. After I got a graduate degree, I headed out to California. No one else in my peer group ever did such things. And I clearly didn't do them because of some God-ordained pull on my life. I did them because I was compensating for my wounds—wounds that, by and large, I had inflicted on myself.

I, like many others, sought the alluring *P* words of *prestige, power, profit,* and *popularity.* And every bit of what I got came from the biggest *p* word of all—*pain.* Fortunately for me, I found a wife and a faith, and I began to experience the healing necessary for balance. These factors prevented me from taking all the fuel of my past and poisoning myself with it.

There have been some near misses along the way, but I've managed not to sacrifice my family or my faith for the applause of the crowd. I'd love to tell you that is because of my fine character, but it is much more because of my wife, Sandy, who has held me accountable and helped me to remain balanced and centered. I think I'll put on her tombstone, "She was not impressed." I love her far more today and our love for each other is much stronger today than when we first married.

You may think that my account of my early days reveals only some very superficial wounds. I agree. They were nothing compared with what many people have to endure. I have never known the evil abuse of a parent. I don't compare my problems with those who have had to endure emotional, physical, or sexual abuse. Those are real wounds, not like my superficial ones. The sad thing about wounds is that no matter how superficial, we have a way of infecting them and turning them into something much more than they were. That is what I did. Rather than be grateful for what I had, I longed for what I did not have. It was early that I started to seek the 25 percent more that would make me feel fulfilled.

WOUNDED WARRIORS

I am not the first person who has ever used wounds as fuel for success. Most people long for deep meaning, but they go after it through superficial means. They follow a typical pattern of others who win—wounded warriors who strive to become wounded winners. Some way or other, these wounded warriors have been hurt early in life. It might have happened through neglect or overindulgence. It might have been because of truly horrible abuse or some form of imagined abuse. It doesn't really matter. Wounds are wounds, and if individuals feel wounded, as I said before, they attempt to medicate the wounds.

People medicate by mainlining their self-administered adrenaline of accomplishment. They may get high on the cocaine of achievement. Or drunk on the wine of winning. Or strong through the steroids of success. Or numbed by the opium of order and compulsive control. Whatever the drug of choice, wounded warriors share one common cause—the removal of pain, the medication of the hurting soul. Unfortunately, they inevitably end up wounding themselves all over again. And not only do they hurt themselves, but they injure all of the people who love and support them.

Are you wounded, too? Perhaps your heartache is driving

you to higher and higher levels of success. Maybe you're seeking anesthesia through a misguided mission or the acquisition of money, both without regard for the meaning behind what you do. If you are a wounded warrior, you have three choices:

1. You can medicate the wounds. It doesn't matter what your drug of choice, whether it is workaholism or alcoholism; what you choose to use as medication will eventually become your self-administered poison.
2. You can lick the wounds. Those who choose this route wallow in self-pity, waiting for a handout, losing at everything, while they blame everybody else for their misfortune. Licking wounds always leaves a bitter aftertaste.
3. You can resolve the wounds and allow your sources of weakness to become the foundation of your greatest strengths.

Clearly, item three is the only practical and wise alternative for any wounded warrior. If you have been medicating and licking the wounds, it is time to start resolving them. Painful though it may be, the pain is far less than a lifetime of emptiness, full of "if onlys" and "what-ifs."

CONCLUSION

I hope you can see the philosophical guideposts of this book. First, we will look at the issue of the mission and how to win at the one you choose. Second, we will try to put the proper spin on the money issue so that it adds rather than subtracts from your life. Then, we will discuss the meaning that you can derive from it all. This approach will enable you as a fellow struggler not just to win at work but to win in every dimension.

It is never too late to see things from a different perspective. With so many perspectives in our world it is no wonder we become so confused over these key issues. It is never too late to see, know, and accept the truth beyond the superficial ideas of current society. All of us are riding some dead horses, and now is the time to get off.

Summary:
Eight Points to Remember about Success

1. Winning in one endeavor does not make you successful.
2. If the foundation is not right, no win at the top will be able to fill the cracks at the bottom.
3. Most successful people often spend a lifetime overcoming some deficit, some woundedness, from their early years.
4. Less successful businesspeople are more likely to find satisfaction in areas outside work.
5. Success-driven businesspeople find that enough is never enough.
6. Emptiness occurs when there is an imbalance of priorities and a lack of a solid foundation.
7. Winning always comes with a price, but when that price is every relationship you have, the price is too great.
8. If we don't learn from others' mistakes, we learn to make their mistakes.

CHAPTER TWO

The Act and Art of Winning

Whater you are ready to re-
move yourself from the dead horse that has gotten you nowhere but frustrated, you are ready to ride like a winner.
What does it take to be a winner? Losers sit back and com-
plain that they didn't have the right parents or opportunities
or they were dealt with unfairly at every turn in life. Losers
will tell you that the favored ones end up winning. Losers are
wrong. In fact, some of the most incredible winners have
come from some of the most incredibly horrible situations,
but they have risen to the challenge and beaten the odds. You
can, too.

You may think of yourself as a loser. That's a problem, of
course, but one that you can overcome. You may feel that you
are in a dead-end job or that you are too weak or unskilled.
You may possess one of the world's largest inferiority com-
plexes, thinking that only geniuses make it to the top of the

organization. You may think that you are up against too many roadblocks and setbacks to ever find success and win.

Nothing could be farther from the truth. All we have to do is get you to move your focus away from all of these things that don't matter and move your focus back to the things that do matter. Below is a list of the things that matter most when it comes to winning. We'll add to the list as we go, compiling a success guide for winners.

NUMBER 1: THE ONLY THING WINNERS ARE UP AGAINST IS THEIR OWN ATTITUDE

The most valuable thing I have ever learned in attempting to win—and the key concept I keep at the forefront of all I do in my work—comes in two parts. Here is the first part:

What you think you are up against is not what you are up against.

You can list every negative you have going against you, and I would tell you that not one matters one bit. You may have convinced yourself that they are the big problems in your life, but they are not and they never will be. What you see as obstacles may be the stepping-stones that lead you to winning. Let me illustrate the best way I can with the story of one of the most successful people I know. She is a hero I think of frequently when I am up against all the odds.

Her name is Joni, and she uses a wheelchair. Now before you write this off as one of those stories where a person with a disability learns to accept their limitations, please read on. Joni was in an accident that left her paralyzed from the shoulders down. Unless we have been there, we cannot know the struggle of living without complete mobility. Mental institutions are strewn with those who could not handle who they had become. Graveyards are marked with tombstones of those who decided they would rather be dead than live a life in a wheelchair. Joni's perseverance is contrasted with the failures of all those who refused to live up to the challenge.

Joni struggled with accepting her plight. She grieved and mourned as she accepted what she was up against. She was no longer independent, could not walk, and could not use her hands. She almost thought that her dreams would never be realized. She wanted to be a writer and illustrate her books. That's not too easy for a person who can't use her hands. If you looked at her in the first few weeks after the accident, you would have found plenty of things to identify as obstacles to her ever fulfilling her dreams.

Sometimes the obvious is not the essential. This young woman did not focus on the obvious. Joni realized the second part of one of the most important lessons of life. Here comes the second part:

The only thing you are up against is your own attitude.

Joni was one of the fortunate ones who discovered that there was something she did have control over: her attitude. Before she started working on her mobility skills, she went to work on her attitude. That really is what all of us are up against: our own attitudes. Someone will always be better off, and someone will always be worse off. It won't matter either way if we have our attitudes working for us rather than against us.

Joni took a strong faith in God and turned that into an attitude of a winner. As a result she has become the inspiration for millions of people. By learning how to hold a pencil or paintbrush in her mouth, Joni has written and illustrated her books, one of which is a favorite of my daughter's. She has painted greeting cards. She has spoken to thousands of people. She has written and recorded songs. In addition she has set up special retreats for families who have concerns with disabilities. Rather than focus on what she is owed, she is giving back. She has the heart and spirit of a winner.

Before I leave the subject of Joni Eareckson Tada, I want you to know about an incredible experience I had at one of her retreats. I was asked to deliver a message from my book *Faith That Hurts, Faith That Heals* about Christians with illnesses never being second-class Christians in the eyes of God. Before my talk, there was a talent show. All of the kids performed, some from their wheelchairs, some on crutches. Some had talent rarely seen in schools of fine arts. One act was perhaps the most beautiful performance I have seen.

In the middle of the talent show, a woman, about twenty-seven, began to dance to the music "Wind Beneath My Wings." As she proceeded with the dance, she was joined by her younger sister who has Down's syndrome. Every movement between the two was as well synchronized as any Olympic ice dancing team has ever achieved. It was art at a rare level of performance beauty. Its real beauty came from knowledge of how many hours had gone into preparation, hours that were shared by two sisters whose love glowed from their faces and the final embrace of love and acceptance. I saw in that moment that the young girl with Down's syndrome was indeed the more fortunate because she was the recipient of a rare love that few of us will experience from another person. Love, acceptance, engagement, and delight—all came flowing from a wonderfully talented and gifted young girl. From her face radiated the attitude of thankfulness and joy. Others with much more opportunities and skills have failed to achieve the level of her competence because of an attitude that keeps them back. Her attitude was not unlike that of Joni's: "Take what you have and with God's help, do the best with it."

Attitude is very difficult to cultivate if it is not there. As

WINNING AT WORK

an employer, I find that much of my job involves trying to discover who has a profoundly positive attitude and who has lost it. Several times I have reviewed key indicator reports, reports that point to the direction an operation is going and identify when an operation has begun to decline. Looking into what happened to previously successful operations, I find that the person in charge no longer has the will or desire to win. The attitude is shot. For some reason, the person decides that failure is inevitable. When a new person with a new attitude is brought in, it is amazing how the same operation that failed in the same location can now succeed. All the resources remain the same, except for the most valuable resource of a desire to win and an attitude to make that win happen.

NUMBER 2: THOSE WHO FOCUS FINISH STRONG

Winners not only have a great attitude; they also focus on the essentials and leave the rest undone. It is common that a boy in high school who has excelled in many things is elected Most Likely to Succeed. But frequently, that person never reaches full potential because he has too many talents in too many areas. He is unable to focus on one area and develop it into a successful career. On the other hand, the little guy no one pays any attention to, the guy who hammers away at his computer all weekend and cracks the code to Fort Knox, ends up running a computer software company and makes millions. Why? Because he was never confused about what he loved and where his talents rested. He was focused, centered, and directed.

The focused person is able to turn down needless invitations. If you are a leader of an operation or an organization, you will be invited over and over again to get busy on a thousand different projects that won't seem to matter at all whether you win or lose. Well, they will matter because if you accept enough invitations to be interrupted from your focus on priorities, all your energy will go into the mundane, and you will not have succeeded at achieving the main goal. Busyness will destroy your focus on the day-to-day routine you must follow to accomplish great things.

It's not only little things that destroy our focus. There are some very dangerous big ones that mess us up, also. California can produce some rather unique people such as Dean. Dean was the highly respected financial manager for a number of artists in the entertainment business. Besides having a brilliant mind for numbers, Dean was a likable guy. His personality naturally drew people to him. He had several clients of international fame, and they gave him free rein with their personal fortunes. Dean had provided them with years of excellent advice and service. They trusted him implicitly. He took care of their banking, their bills, their investments, their taxes, and their accounting.

Dean's financial services didn't come cheaply, and as you can imagine, the two homes he shared with his wife and two children were beautifully designed and lavishly appointed. One overlooked the Pacific Ocean; the other was perched high in the Hollywood Hills. They were filled with fine art, elegant furnishings, and state-of-the-art electronic equipment.

When the two FBI agents came to the door of the Laguna Beach house, Dean's wife, Katy, was completely surprised. Why on earth would the FBI be looking for Dean?

"He's out of the country," she explained calmly.

"When will he be back?"

"Next week."

Dean didn't come back for two months. He kept telling Katy he was tied up in contract negotiations in Europe. She was beginning to have serious doubts about his story, particularly when the IRS joined the search for Dean. When he finally returned, he was immediately arrested and jailed on charges of embezzlement and fraud. Once Katy heard the facts about Dean, which included involvements with a couple of high-priced call girls, she filed for divorce. Today Dean is serving time at a minimum security state prison.

Although he had earned a handsome income for twenty years and had kept his nose completely clean in the process, Dean's access to huge amounts of money had finally gnawed away at his moral resistance. He changed his focus from what he had and had to do to what he didn't have and what he felt he was entitled to. Like most humans, he never really thought he had enough cash. And with his skills, it was far too easy to transfer funds from someone else's account into his own. Before long, he got used to the surplus, and he wanted more. The easy money was as addictive to Dean as any drug. And like drug abuse, it destroyed his business, bankrupted his resources, ripped apart his family, ruined his reputation, and devastated his future. It couldn't have been worth it.

Dean was a winner for a long time, but he allowed his focus to change. He broke his own rules. And today he's nothing but a big-time loser. That's what happens when you lose your focus. When you look more to the winnings than winning, you get unfocused and out of balance.

Take the time to ask yourself where your focus is. Are you focused? Are you allowing distractions of money or power to distort your focus? Are you pointed like an arrow toward what will provide you with the most satisfaction? If you are, you have a chance at being a winner. If you aren't, you won't win, and you will hate the process you have to go through to work so hard to achieve so little. The focused individual accomplishes much and is able to do it over the long haul.

Before we move on, let's take a few minutes to clear up the focus in your career. Answer the following questions.

The Act and Art of Winning

1. What is the most essential area that needs your constant focus? (It is the one thing that will ensure failure if neglected.)

2. If you went through the process of focusing on this one area, ensuring that it was accomplished, what would be the biggest benefit to you and your career?

3. What are the five most prevalent interruptions to your focus? (In other words, if you are going to be distracted from achieving your goal, what are the five things that most likely will get your attention to your detriment?)

4. What is the thing you like to do the most that has the least to do with accomplishing your goals? (For example, do you like to talk to fellow workers during office hours? Do you like to talk on the phone? Do you spend too much time on sports? Do you like to shop but spend too much money on items you really can't afford?)

These four issues, if you consider them deeply, may unlock your potential to focus on the priorities that will lead to winning. Once you are able to focus, you begin the process of winning. Beginning is a major accomplishment since so many fear failure and never try. The next step enables you to make your win last for the long term, and it involves integrity.

NUMBER 3: WINNING WITH INTEGRITY ISN'T EASY; WINNING WITHOUT IT IS IMPOSSIBLE

Integrity is the steadfast adherence to a strict moral or ethical code. People with it have established a set of boundaries that they refuse to cross. They are unimpaired in the decision-making process, knowing certain things are acceptable and certain things are not. Their integrity enables them to make sound decisions. If you have integrity, you are a whole person, undivided by passions. You are in control. Sadly, most of the people I have known who have achieved great things have done so without integrity, and the end result of all their winnings and success has been one of the following: (1) loss of it all, (2) public humiliation, (3) disgrace of the family, (4) public rejection and ridicule by the family, (5) illness and death from sexually transmitted diseases, or (6) loss of freedom.

My wife and I owned a swimwear company for eight years in Southern California. Although it was great fun traveling to photo shoots on tropical islands, it was a business full of stress and competitive drive. We were in great debt each season, and my wife fought hard to keep the company expanding every year. When we adopted our daughter, we knew it was time to sell. We were relieved to have such a great excuse to get out of such a tough industry. So we put it up for sale and sold it. Twice.

The first time we sold it to a man in the industry who had a much more successful company than ours. At least it appeared that way. He was always doing nice things for others in the industry. He never appeared to be under any kind of stress. No one could figure out where his money came from because he seemed to spend much more than the other companies of his size. When the industry was in a slump, he just kept going as if nothing was a problem. It seemed he had so much money that selling our company to him would be the logical decision. So we did.

He made the first installment on the company of $100,000, and the check was good. Before the second installment could come, the FBI stepped in and arrested him. As of this writing, he is still in prison for conducting a check-kiting scheme that involved over one hundred bank accounts and thousands of checks. We got the company back and sold it again. The check kiter had gotten it all wrong. Somehow he had come to believe that the look of success on the outside was the key to a life of success. I suspect if he had it to do over again, he would have preferred to go through the painful process of bankruptcy instead of the humiliation of becoming a felon. Many people with integrity have to file for bankruptcy. There are no felons who walk into prison with integrity. Some walk out with it, but there are some much easier ways to learn it than by incarceration.

Although the newspapers are full of stories of unethical businesspeople, I have been amazed to find just the opposite in the everyday practice of business. The key ingredient to long-term success is integrity. Just from the practical standpoint of not having to spend your time looking over your shoulder, you can make better decisions. People with integrity have peace of mind, and they rest well knowing that they are doing their best and that it is enough. The soundness of mind that comes from integrity is always destroyed by succumbing to the temptations of ill-gotten gains. One way to everyday successes is to start each day making integrity a priority.

Let's take a few minutes to check up on your level of integrity.

1. All of us are a little different in public from the way we are in private. Think of the things that are completely different about you that would allow someone to say you are a phony or a fraud.

WINNING AT WORK

2. Has telling the truth become a problem for you? Can you think of a time when telling a lie caused you more pain than if you had told the truth?

3. List ten important values or principles that you attempt to adhere to in all your business practices. (These should be things like honesty, fairness, and quality.)

If you really believe in these ten concepts or principles, you might want to transfer them to another piece of paper and keep them on your desk, or better yet hang them on your wall, so others will know the self-imposed rules you are trying to live by.

NUMBER 4: A SOUND BODY MAKES FOR A SOUND MIND

Not only do winners maintain a life of moral and ethical fitness, they also find a way to stay in shape physically. There are a few exceptions to this in this day, but most of the people I am around look fit and are fit. The exceptions never exercise, drink a lot, and smoke like an old train, but I don't think they are really enjoying themselves the way they could be if they would break a few habits and take up a new lifestyle. In my dealings I have a hard time respecting a person's decisions regarding business if it is obvious he makes poor decisions about his own body. If a person is irresponsible in her personal life, there is a good chance I will see similar irresponsibility at work. What I admire about people who are fit is discipline.

Discipline is one of the success characteristics that can be developed. If you are not able to get to a gym four times a week, you can still be disciplined enough to take a ten-minute walk before you leave for work. If you don't have ten minutes now, you can be disciplined enough to wake yourself up ten minutes earlier.

I think that personal discipline is somehow rewarded in the workplace. One reward is a more relaxed and clear mind. The other is the respect of others. No one ever loses when a winner at work is determined to keep the body in as good a shape as the mind needs to be to win.

Let's take a look at what you need to do to develop a sounder body.

1. What one eating habit, if eliminated, would make a major improvement in your weight?

2. What exercise would you enjoy doing the most if you got back into the habit of exercising?

3. What person as a partner would most likely help you keep yourself in shape?

4. What is the one thought or attitude that keeps you from doing for your body what you know you need to do?

5. What could you do to change the shape of that attitude to change the shape of your body?

NUMBER 5: MAKE FAITH YOUR FOOTHOLD

Once your body is in good shape and fit, it will be of no benefit if you don't have faith as a strong foothold. Mountain climbers know the importance of a strong foothold. It can be the difference between life and death. When faith is our foothold in our personal and professional lives, it can also be the difference between life and death. When I have hidden my faith, I have always been disappointed in myself. When I have tried to share it subtly, it has always brought me great satisfaction. Last year when I gave my acceptance speech for Entrepreneur of the Year Award, I told the audience that all of us in my company had seen the company as a gift from God and we had tried to honor Him in all we do. A year later when I was a judge of that same competition, the emcee referred to my speech when the judges were being introduced. What I had hesitated to say had been remembered the most.

When my company has been through tough times, my faith has kept me going. I know God loves me personally and has a plan for me, even if my company goes out of business. That faith allows me to make some bold decisions that others might not make if they felt that God was distant and impersonal. My foothold is my faith, and all I do comes from that strong foothold. When my company did poorly for a while, I gathered my associates together and said that if we were going to go out of business or just through a tough time, we wanted to come out better people, not worse. We made a commitment to each other not to let the stress break us apart. We lived up to that commitment. We allowed the difficulties and weaknesses to focus us on the strength of God.

The security of a strong faith allows people to make strong decisions. Those who are not strongly rooted in faith become like a raft on the ocean in a storm. You feel tossed about, to and fro, wondering if you will make it, wondering if you will stay afloat. I don't know of a more miserable way to live, questioning every decision you make, wondering if you have done the right thing. With faith, you don't have to worry as much about doing the right thing. You know that if you remain faithful, God will work out your mistakes into something good for His purpose and yours. That kind of faith sure takes off a lot of pressure.

Since there are those who have faith and those who don't, and those who have it seem to get along much better than those who don't, let's take a few minutes to examine some of the potential causes of people turning against God or away from faith.

1. Often people lose their faith over a major loss in their lives. They feel that there must not be a God if something so horrible would be allowed to happen. They feel God betrayed them. Can you identify some major disappointment in your life that causes you to question the existence of God?

2. Often people reject God because they were rejected by an older adult, especially a parent. Was there something in your childhood that caused you to feel rejected by people and by God?

3. Bitterness toward another person seems to block out awareness of God. Often those who struggle in their faith find that they are holding a grudge against people they should love. Is there someone you need to forgive?

4. If you are going to win at work without losing at love, you are going to need the help of God. Take a few minutes to compose a prayer of dedication. Ask God to grant you success with meaning in your work and in your personal life.

NUMBER 6: WINNERS CREATE INNER PEACE AND SERENITY

A strong faith can also provide a sense of security that has other benefits also.

A few days ago I was with one of my board members, and we were about to negotiate a $1 million investment in our company. The people we were meeting with were very successful, tough businesspeople, and the chances of our getting what we wanted seemed slim. I sat during the meeting, allowing the board member to have complete control. There were many times I wanted to blurt out something to make our case, but I didn't. I sat there and let this man produce long segments of quiet. They were uncomfortable times for everyone in the room. He seemed to be the master of them. He had the ability to sit there, make a point, and quietly and confidently wait for the other people to blink. Blink they did, and we ended up with exactly what we had hoped for at the beginning of the meeting.

The man I am describing is nothing like the business tycoons portrayed in movies who are six feet eight and overpower a room from their size alone. He is a small man whose power is in his lack of anxiety and his ability to stay in control of himself. His estate is huge because he has learned to silently wait. The hard charger is not always the one who succeeds, especially when it is anxiety that keeps the person moving. When you have an inner peace about your work, people see it, and they are drawn to it. It creates respect and cooperation. Few people wouldn't want to have someone who is cool under pressure either be on their team or run their team.

They key is finding a way to calm yourself down when you need to be cool and calm. Some people do it by counting backward. Others do it by counting the things they are thankful for. Others consider the next potential move by the negotiator and play out the negotiation in advance much like a chess game. Still others flash a big red stop sign in their heads when they are about to speak, forcing themselves to say nothing until they have waited an extra few seconds and thought it through. Let's consider some points that will indicate your security and ability to show calmness under pressure.

1. When you are anxious in a meeting, what are some of the things you worry about or focus on?

2. Think of the place where you grew up that brought you the most happiness, a place where you felt at home, safe and secure. Describe that beautiful place.

3. The next time you are anxious, attempt to think of that place and allow yourself to get caught up in the mood of that past place of peace rather than your current situation. Describe another way of thinking that you could use when you start to become anxious during a negotiation. How could you distract your anxiety while still maintaining your focus on the meeting?

4. A strong faith plays a vital role in maintaining serenity and peace. If we feel we have all the control and God has none, we are carrying around an awful lot of stress and responsibility. When we trust God and turn all of our concerns over to Him, we are relieved of a tremendous burden. Write a statement that you can memorize and recall under stress. Make this statement a sincere surrender of your work and efforts, trusting God to do what you cannot do.

NUMBER 7: WINNERS ARE LEARNERS

When I find peace and serenity, I am more comfortable and motivated with improving myself, sharpening my skills, and expanding my vision. I don't know anyone in business who is successful and doesn't read a lot. I'm sure some nonreaders who are successful are out there; I just haven't met them. I read about the industry I am in to stay up with trends. I read about my competition to make sure that I'm not overlooking some part of the market. Reading is a major part of my battle plan to win. I try to be the good student I never was in school.

I like to have people around me who are readers. They provide me with information I don't have and a sense of confidence that within the organization we have informed problem solvers who are always increasing their value through increased knowledge. If you are not at the top, one of the ways up there can be through reading. Use your spare time to find articles that relate to the operation, clip them out, and send them up the ladder. It is a valid way to go through the chain of command and to the top to be noticed. I have never known a CEO who hated being informed by an employee several levels down.

Reading is important for ongoing learning, but seminars occasionally provide the right excuse to get you and the employees out of the office for an educational outing together. We attend everything from motivational meetings to negotiation seminars. As a result, we are much better leaders and managers today than when we started the company. We are more valuable resources due to our training.

The fact that you are reading this book shows that you are a learner trying to hone some new skills or develop some new ideas of a winner. Take a few minutes to write down four activities you could do over the next six months that would make you a more valuable resource for your company.

1.

2.

3.

4.

NUMBER 8: NEVER ALLOW THE PAST TO RUIN YOUR FUTURE

It is always sad to watch people experience success and then watch them destroy all that they have accomplished in about half the time it took to succeed. Within some people is a self-destructive mode that sabotages all that they do. Often the source is some form of guilt from a past that wasn't exactly perfect. If it isn't guilt, it is a chip of resentment that continues to pop up on the person's shoulder. It is such a loss to see people with baggage from their past unpack their bags in the current job and allow all their problems to destroy another opportunity.

If you have a pattern of getting a job and leaving or being asked to leave within a short time, it shows that you have a lot going for you to be able to be employed. It also shows that there are probably some unmet personal needs and some issues from the past that need to be resolved so you don't reproduce them in every new job you take. I think many careers could have been saved with the assistance of a counselor. Let's take a few minutes to determine some issues that might be there for you and a counselor to resolve.

WINNING AT WORK

1. Do you commonly have run-ins with people at work that result in your having to leave the job? Is there a common thread in these events? What is it?

2. When you look back at your past, do you see a pattern of conflict and running? Do you see yourself escaping every time there is pressure or disagreement? Does it feel that sometimes you are almost looking for trouble as an excuse to leave the job? What part of your past do you feel might have influenced this pattern? Did you learn this habit very young? Write out what you think plays an important factor in ongoing conflict at work.

3. Many times people become needy and out of control at work because their needs are not being met at home. Below, take the time to write about how you plan to get the following needs met away from work so you will have fewer problems at work.

Physical:

Mental:

Emotional:

Social:

Spiritual:

Work this plan for a month and see if work isn't a more enjoyable place. See if people start to notice a change in your attitude and the way you interact with them.

The Act and Art of Winning

NUMBER 9: CELEBRATE THE SUCCESS OF OTHERS

Being envious of where others have gotten only makes you look small and keeps you stuck in your current role. Bringing everyone else down to your level will result in everyone you know achieving mediocrity rather than greatness. Most people do it that way and prevent themselves from achieving great things. There is a different way that produces much better results. Rather than envy the success of others, celebrate it, encourage it, and ensure that it happens.

Long before I ran a company, I was a number two person in different organizations. I thought I was a pretty good number two. My drive was a bit much for some of my supervisors, but I never wanted to walk over them. I wanted them to succeed so I could move up right along with them. That strategy worked. The better I did, the better they did. My salary and bonuses went up as did theirs. Everybody won. Finally, there was a parallel spot with my supervisor. Eventually, those I had worked for worked for me.

Once I had people working for me, I continued to celebrate their success. I never wanted anyone held back. I didn't care if people were so productive that they made more money than I did. We were a team, and when anyone on the team did well, we all did well. The best way to move yourself up is to move up the people under you and over you. It allows you to have a team spirit and fosters outstanding performance. You will look mature to the other workers. As you celebrate the success of others, there will always be someone looking out for your best interests.

Let's stop long enough to analyze how this principle could add to your success.

WINNING AT WORK

1. Identify the one person in your organization who seems to have the most potential to win, whether the person is above or below you.

2. What is the one thing you could do to further that person's career?

3. How could you communicate to that person your dedication to his or her success?

4. What could you plan to do as a means of celebrating the success of one of your associates?

Celebrating another person's success doesn't have to be elaborate or complicated. It can be something as simple as daily identifying someone who needs a boost, paying a compliment, or offering support and giving that person what is needed.

NUMBER 10: BE ACCOUNTABLE

This principle of a winner is a tough one. No one really likes to be accountable to anyone else. That is especially true of people who seek the independence found in running their own companies or operations. From our teens we seek independence, not accountability. Yet accountable relationships are like a rudder. Without them, you will most definitely stray off course. Submitting yourself to accountable relationships will keep you on course and keep others on the course with you.

If you are married, you need to be accountable to your husband or wife. That means revealing to that person the tough things about who you are. Sharing your doubts and weaknesses and fears will build your relationship. It is living up to the commitment made at the time of the marriage. Too many people in business lead two separate lives. They have a professional life that is kept completely out of touch from a personal life. Then they have a personal life that doesn't really match who they are at work. Accountability allows the two to merge to become one. There are congruency and consistency that produce greater results.

One of the saddest things I have seen in business is the family man who has wonderful children and a great wife, but he runs around on them on every trip. I have seen men whose spouses thought they were faithful; I have heard those men speak of prostitutes and affairs as if all men were entitled to them. I have watched those men be found out, families destroyed, hearts crushed—all from a lack of accountability. Be accountable to your spouse.

Additionally, be accountable to someone other than your spouse. Find a friend you can confess every sin and mistake to. I have that in Jim Burns. There is nothing I wouldn't tell him, and that keeps my heart clean before people and before God. He has complete freedom to ask me about lust, greed, selfishness, attitudes, and busyness. I respect his wisdom and judgment, and I believe I am on track today because of his guidance. If you don't have a person to whom you are accountable, get one. It may take some searching, but you will find the person if you are determined to be accountable.

1. In what ways do you assert your independence from your commitments, ways that you must keep secret from others?

2. Name three people who are possible candidates for developing an accountability relationship.

3. Name the one characteristic of your life that you would like to change, the thing that you would allow another person to hold you accountable for.

4. Name the greatest benefit you can think of from developing greater accountability to your spouse and one other person.

NUMBER 11: BE REALISTIC ABOUT STRENGTHS AND WEAKNESSES

There is one last characteristic of a winner that I want to mention briefly. A winner is able to make a realistic appraisal of personal strengths and weaknesses so that goals are realistic. Unrealistic expectations of yourself lead only to frustration and failure. If the sum of your intelligence and skill adds up to having the ability to be a janitor, be a janitor. But be the best janitor ever. Serve the community well in that position. Save a little money and seek advice in investing it. Even as a janitor, you can win and end up with a large nest egg for retirement.

Often people with limited skills see someone who has made it and expect to be able to do it, also—and quickly. When they find they don't have the talent or the blessing of God to accomplish their goals, they feel like failures. In despair they drink heavily or lash out in anger. They destroy what talent they do have because of their deep despair.

Be realistic. Take a survey of your talent, and be sure that the mission you want to achieve is one that is achievable. Let's take a few minutes to assess the track you are on to make sure you are on the right mission.

1. What are your greatest strengths that allow you to excel in the workplace?

The Act and Art of Winning

2. When people compliment you, what do they identify as positive traits about your character?

3. At work, are you affirmed in what you do or constantly criticized?

4. Do you want your life to be characterized in the end as you are living it now?

5. What one area of your work is a weakness that needs development?

6. What can you do to develop that weakness into a strength?

7. Has anyone ever told you that your expectations were unrealistic?

8. Find a person who believes that about you, and ask for details of why the person thinks you are unrealistic.

9. Write down one goal for your life that beyond a shadow of a doubt you know you could accomplish.

10. If you accomplished that goal and were considered a winner in that area, what would your major contribution have been to this world? Would there be lasting results?

In summary, if you want to be a winner, you can be. Or you can reach too high and attempt too much, guaranteeing

WINNING AT WORK

that you will lose. Don't allow yourself to reach for more than you can handle. Win small before you try to win big. Commit to excellence at whatever you do. If it is the least job in a company, let it be said of you that you do that job better than any other person could.

In addition to excellence, winners are committed to service. Those who succeed so they can serve find fulfillment and meaning that others who seek power will never have. See all that you do as a means of God allowing you to influence and help more people. By doing that, you will develop a reputation and a heritage for your family. You will be laying down footprints that will be a pleasure to follow.

Winning is up to you. What you win and how you win are in your hands. Choose to win, but never at the expense of another person, your family, or your faith. Setting up these parameters of winning allows you to find and achieve a life mission that is far more than just winning. It becomes a mission of contribution, which in every respect is a mission of love.

Summary:
Eleven Marks of a Winner

1. Winners realize that the only thing they are up against is their own attitude, so they maintain a positive one.
2. Winners focus on priorities and refuse to allow busyness and distractions to take them off their focus.
3. Winners live a life of integrity on the job and off.
4. Winners keep their bodies in as good a shape and fit as possible.
5. Winners develop and maintain a strong faith.
6. Winners create an inner peace and serenity.
7. Winners never stop learning.
8. Winners don't allow their past to ruin their future.

9. Winners celebrate the success of others.
10. Winners maintain accountability.
11. Winners are realistic about their strengths and weaknesses.

CHAPTER THREE

Seven Costly Mistakes

We all make mistakes. The bigger the responsibility, the bigger the mistakes we are likely to make. In my company we encourage new employees to make mistakes, the bigger the better. We know that if people are out there making mistakes, they won't be just playing it safe. We want people to try hard to win, make mistakes in the process, learn from them, and then get on with the job.

One of my employees made a mistake that cost our company about $35,000. He asked me if I was going to fire him. I told him no, not after we had just spent $35,000 in on-the-job training.

Mistakes are part of every person's job. They are inevitable, but there are certain mistakes that we don't have to make because they are more mistakes of the heart. I've described the costly mistakes that must be avoided to continue to win at work as well as at love. They are costly to everyone and even deadly to many.

NUMBER 1: BLIND AMBITION

What is blind ambition? Entire books have been written on the subject—the most notable one by former White House elitist John Dean, who learned some hard lessons about his own ambitions during the Watergate scandal. In short, having blind ambition means wanting to have the appearance of greatness versus wanting to be a truly great person who does great things.

---

*Blind ambition
is an ego trip,
not a mission.*

Several dangers are associated with this particular mistake. For one thing, ambition at all costs will cost you valuable people. Bright, thoughtful people eventually see through the facade that thinly disguises the overly ambitious individual. Before long, the real priorities begin to make themselves known. These are some of the ingredients that form the attitude of the blindly ambitious person:

- Nothing will stand in the way of my success.
- People are to be used, not valued.
- The ends justify the means.

- The winner takes all.
- Those who don't support my success are enemies.

Blindly ambitious people develop systems without accountability because they don't want to be scrutinized. They are usually hiding something—the blindness in blind ambition is imposed on everyone. Like dysfunctional families, the people who surround these individuals are forced into a state of denial, enablement, and codependency.

Of course, the ultimate result of unbridled ambition is personal emptiness. Remember the man I mentioned in chapter 1 who received an award for outstanding achievement but had no one to celebrate with him? The blindly ambitious are lonely, isolated by their own agendas, and trapped in their self-involvement. They may have accomplished their mission. They may have all kinds of money. But life holds no magic for them; they are blind to the real meaning of their existence.

The flashes in the pan, the screaming streaks of light across the business field of play, are those who are blinded by their own ambition. They start strong, head strong, and finish empty. In their path are strewn all those who helped them but received only a raw deal for their assistance. There is nothing wrong with ambition, but when it drives you beyond the ethical line and humane treatment, it eventually kills you and destroys your soul. If you have ever been accused of having blind ambition, you need to bring it into check as quickly as possible. That will come only if you are willing to become accountable to another and hear the truth about yourself.

One final note: people with blind ambition who bring it under control are often the ones who accomplish the most over a lifetime with relationships and freedoms still in place.

NUMBER 2: MANIPULATION OF PEOPLE

Like the blindly ambitious person, the individual who manipulates people, either at home or at work, produces only temporary results. Instead of building a team, these men and women have a "divide and conquer" strategy. You may recognize some of their tactics. Manipulators

- pit one person against another.
- withhold information and use it as a control device.
- motivate through fear and intimidation.
- use shallow flattery as a ploy.
- explode when they are thwarted.
- indirectly and dishonestly address difficult issues, using underhanded means to get their way.
- reduce people rather than reward them.

Families in which manipulative people operate are not only unhealthy; they are often abusive. Companies that practice manipulative management reflect abnormally high employee turnover, inner-office turbulence, poor morale, and disloyalty throughout the ranks. Most people who do it don't intend to, but the pattern is easy to follow.

Every person adopts a style of management he or she sees as the easiest way to produce results. Most believe their preferred style is motivational whether by word or by money. Almost all managers are proud of their ability to motivate the troops to get results. If you ask them how they do it, they will most likely tell you of all the positive and powerful things they do to move people into action. What they don't tell you is that when things are not going so well, when results don't appear readily enough, they resort to a secondary style of management. The secondary style comes out when the pressure is on, and that style is probably going to be manipulative.

I think everyone will have to use a small amount of manipulation in the career, but the more you must resort to it, the less likely you will be able to attract a talented team of followers who will be loyal and long on commitment. Manipulators aren't team players, and they don't win like motivators do.

NUMBER 3: PRIDE

Pride has been said to be the original sin, and it takes many forms. Sometimes, it is evidenced by an arrogant manner. In other cases, pride is seen in an insecure, self-effacing manner. Insecure people are just as proud as pompous people —in both cases, they are focused on what people think of them.

Both in business and in family life, pride gets in the way when men and women

- refuse to listen.
- refuse to try things another way.
- refuse to admit wrongs.
- refuse to start over.
- refuse to face facts.
- refuse to acknowledge others' accomplishments.
- refuse to keep up with outside change.
- refuse to negotiate.
- refuse to share success.
- refuse to say, "I'm sorry."

Pride ultimately stands in the way of teamwork because it alienates rather than brings together. It stands in the way of success because two heads are nearly always better than one, and teams often succeed where individuals fail.

People who fall in love with someone else's idea more than their own are the real winners. Even Olympic champions who have worked all their lives to be on the winner's platform had coaches who helped them get there. And the "thank you" speeches at awards ceremonies always include references to those less-visible individuals who have made quiet but irreplaceable contributions to a successful mission.

Perhaps the most valuable business lesson my parents taught me was that pride comes on strong right before a major fall or failure. When I look back on what I have accomplished, it was at those times when pride and arrogance crept in that I did the least or destroyed the most. The new wave of management is not a prideful empire but, instead, a humble system of servant leaders motivating followers to greatness.

NUMBER 4: SHAME

What causes shame, and how does it get in the way of success? In some families, shame is used as a means of control, and children learn very early in life that they are unworthy of good things. Whether the parents are fanatical about discipline or highly authoritarian, a childhood in which shame is a continuous factor can begin a self-destructive process.

Whether our families made us overly sensitive to shame or not, all of us have failed in some way, and we have things in the past we wish weren't there. Those shameful incidents or passages of time may cause us to sabotage our positive accomplishments because of the following reasons:

- We feel we don't deserve good things. We may have been abused or mistreated in childhood, and we internalized the belief that people like us don't deserve the good things in life. Therefore, shame-filled people may feel uncomfortable with success.

- We feel we should pay penance for the past. People who are ashamed tend to go beyond feeling guilty for specific sins that can be forgiven. We often feel guilty for who we are, how we are, or the kind of people we see ourselves to be. Therefore, life itself may be seen as unending penance.
- We believe God is going to punish us. When bad things happen to shame-filled people, we often believe we deserve them, and we see them as God's way of punishing us. When good things happen, we have a hard time enjoying the good fortune because we feel it is undeserved.
- We haven't learned to celebrate. It is hard to celebrate successes (whether personal or business related) when we feel that we are the kind of people who do not deserve them.
- We can't see ourselves as successful. When we catch a glimpse of ourselves as successful, the image is not familiar. Shame and success do not comfortably coexist. It is a costly mistake to allow shame-related issues to go unconfronted in our lives. Overcoming shame issues is essential if we are going to be winners.

One of the unique qualities of Christianity is that it doesn't require us to be good in order to have a relationship with God. In fact, the first thing we have to understand in order to embrace Christianity is that we aren't really able to keep all the rules, but God has chosen to forgive us and love us anyway. We believe that the price of our shame has already been paid by Jesus, through His death and resurrection.

Once that account is settled, and you see that God has forgiven you, it is easier for you to forgive yourself. And that's exactly what you have to do. Let's examine the helpful steps to shame reduction.

The first step in ridding yourself of shame is determining whether you're feeling true shame or experiencing some kind of false guilt that you've carried around since childhood. Guilt is felt over a specific incident that can be acknowledged and corrected. Shame is a general sense of unworthiness that does not directly relate to any particular wrong you can correct.

The second step in overcoming shame is forgiving yourself for whatever you've truly done wrong. You begin by acknowledging the wrongdoing to yourself and whoever else appropriate (persons harmed by your actions, authorities, and so on). Ask forgiveness from God and those you have wronged. Receive the forgiveness, and whenever possible make amends.

The third step in removing shame from your life is understanding why you did wrong in the first place. There are often underlying factors that influence a person to do wrong. These do not excuse wrong behavior, but if you do not deal with the source of your inclinations, you may repeat past errors. If you do not know what contributes to your behavior, consider seeking counsel from someone who has experience in the field.

You may not have done anything wrong in particular, but you still feel something is wrong with you. If you cannot rid yourself of shame or identify specific reasons for your negative attitude toward yourself, seek professional help.

The fourth step in getting rid of shame is making a commitment never to repeat past sins. You must be willing to take responsibility for your actions and moral choices regardless of the negative influences that may have contributed to your past sinful ways. You must determine to do whatever it takes to make sure you go in a different direction. This takes God's help, but He is more than willing to supply it.

The fifth step out of shame is to keep short accounts with

yourself, forgive yourself on a daily basis, ask God to forgive you, and continue to grow.

---

*Who you are today
is far more important
than any misdeed
you have done in the past.*

NUMBER 5: FEAR

During the worst years of the Great Depression, Franklin Roosevelt told the American people, "The only thing we have to fear is fear itself." Arthur Wellesley, the duke of Wellington, once said, "The only thing I am afraid of is fear." Francis Bacon is quoted as saying, "Nothing is terrible except fear itself." It seems that throughout the centuries, great people who have observed life and faced its challenges have come to the same conclusion time after time: it's not the circumstances that threaten to destroy us; it's our own fears that do the damage.

Our first fears originate from our parents and their style of parenting. If they were distant, we may fear being abandoned, and we set up scenarios in adult life that prevent the possibility of anyone abandoning us. If our parents were too dependent on us for their happiness, we may fear we will be smothered, and we find ways to keep our distance as adults.

For those who have the privilege of a happy childhood, they fear that they will not be able to repeat the same experience as adults. Those who have horrible childhoods fear they will repeat the horrors of the past, and they set up patterns to guarantee they won't. How well they adjust to these basic fears and how well they prevent them from dominating their adult lives have a lot to do with their potential as winners.

No one is free from fear, but some individuals courageously respond to it. Others cower in its face and are immobilized. Usually, apart from our typically human fear of death, our most debilitating fears involve

- fear of failure.
- fear of abandonment.
- fear of change.
- fear of loss.

As we consider these possibilities in the clear light of day, we should be able to see that the worst-case scenario is never as bad as our unwillingness to take risks. Fear will prevent us from stretching our limits. It will block us from gaining new ground. It will not allow us to grow and to become more valuable.

Much of our fear has to do with how we appear to others. And the fear of failure is far more detrimental to us in our careers than failure could ever be. It keeps us from trying in the first place. And when we do try and find that we haven't succeeded as well as we'd hoped, fear of looking foolish again refuses to allow us to pick ourselves up, dust ourselves off, and start over again. The Bible says this: "The fear of man brings a snare" (Prov. 29:25). The truth is, anytime we're more concerned about what others think than about doing right, we're headed for that proverbial snare.

Don't be afraid of failing. Instead, keep your eyes on the opportunities before you, and pray for the courage to keep moving forward. An oft-quoted New Testament teaching states that God hasn't given us a spirit that makes us afraid.

He's provided a spirit "of power and of love and of a sound mind" (2 Tim. 1:7).

---

*True winners
are more concerned
about what they will achieve
than about what image they can produce.*

NUMBER 6: LUST

You've heard the story a thousand times. The man is doing well in his business. He's successful and respected. He has the world on a string. Along comes the sweet young thing. Maybe she's a secretary. Or a client. Or an admirer. The man knows better intellectually. He has always said, "That could never happen to me." Maybe he's religious. Maybe he's not. But somewhere along the way, lust overwhelms his resolve. She seduces him. He seduces her. They usually think it's true love, and an affair takes place. And over a period of time, everything the man has worked for begins to slip away. First come the rumors. Then the loss of respect. The family dissolution. The brutal division of property. The emotional and financial ruin.

Was it worth it? Never!

No sexual misdeed has ever been as great as the pain and regret it caused later. And yet many men fall into the lust snare and never get out of it. It may turn into a sex addiction. Or it may simply be a pot of trouble simmering on the back burner, waiting for the right time to boil over.

Seven Costly Mistakes

Although sexual temptation is always there, some factors lead to an attitude of lust. Watch out for the following red flags:

- A need for stress reduction with no healthy ways to reduce it
- A pornography habit that may have begun in childhood
- A need for comfort and no healthy relationship in which to find it
- A need for attention
- An unclear understanding of true intimacy
- An out-of-control fantasy life
- Anger, bitterness, and resentment

It's important to avoid the pitfall of lust before we lose our balance and topple into it. Setting boundaries for ourselves is essential to our sexual self-preservation. If you feel attracted to a certain person, and it would be immoral for you to pursue a relationship, take some steps at the early stage of sexual attraction before trouble begins.

First, stop daydreaming about spending time with the person. Romantic fantasies are just as dangerous as sexual ones.

Second, avoid being alone together. Leave the office door open, and don't schedule lunches for two.

Third, confide in a trusted friend about your attraction for the sake of accountability.

Fourth, don't tell the person about your feelings of attraction. Someone who is interested in you may try to seduce you. If not, the person may sue for harassment.

Fifth, envision the worst-case scenario. The hurt caused by an affair can last for a lifetime.

Sixth, don't take that first step. You may not be able to

avoid the way you feel, but you are responsible for what you do about your feelings.

People with major lust problems usually have major ego problems. Some become convinced that they have needs beyond normal needs. In them exist powerful special needs, there only due to their enormous power and presence. Others have ego problems that go in the other direction. Their self-hatred or insecurity is tempered by the flatteries of romantic involvement or sexual involvement. These people get caught in the lust trap in a search for someone who can convince them that they really are not as unattractive or unlovable as they believe themselves to be.

These people are fools who have fallen for the ploy that dashes brilliant careers on the boulders of instant gratification. This kind of burning lust can be resolved only through the honest and open intimacy that exists between a husband and a wife committed to the growth of the marriage and the growth of each other.

NUMBER 7: LAZINESS

In our modern culture, we find a lot of ways to explain away inappropriate behavior. It is interesting to note that one of the original seven deadly sins was sloth. It was described in these ways:

- Disinclination toward action or labor
- Idleness
- Sluggishness
- Habitual indolence

When you think about it, the definition of sloth sounds a lot like something we call depression. We need to be aware that what looks like laziness may actually be symptomatic of depression, a condition that can last for years. Here are some symptoms of depression:

- Significant weight loss or gain
- Cold hands or feet; sweaty palms
- Assorted aches and pains
- Low energy; slow movements or thoughts
- Irritability
- Poor concentration or memory
- Melancholy mood or crying
- Loss of interest in pleasures, including sex
- Thoughts of death
- Insomnia or sleeping too much

When five or more of these symptoms are present at the same time, particularly thoughts of death, and if they have continued for more than a couple of weeks, it would be wise to see a doctor or a therapist as soon as possible. If you are genuinely depressed, laziness is not your problem. Something else is troubling you, and you need to find out what it is.

Laziness is a different story. It is a very real problem in some lives. Sometimes, it is the result of trying to savor life's meaning without regard for the mission or the need to make money. Other times, it is a destructive habit a person has fallen into. Are you inclined toward laziness?

- Do you often sit idly with nothing to do?
- Do you find ways to avoid tasks?
- Do you feel irritated when you learn that a project is going to need further work?
- Have you ever been accused of being a couch potato?
- Is there a list of things you should have done by now but don't want to deal with?

- Are you a clock-watcher, waiting anxiously for quitting time?
- Do you dump responsibility rather than go to the extra trouble of delegating it?
- Are you fearful that someone will find out about something you should have done and didn't do?
- Do you say to yourself, Why bother? It really isn't important anyway?
- Is leisure time activity (watching television, reading novels, or playing golf) more important to you than getting things done?
- Are you unwilling to pay dues at work?
- Are you unwilling to work on your relationship(s) at home?

If you said yes to more than a couple of these questions, you may have a problem with laziness. How do you change? Just as with any other bad habit, admitting you have a problem is the first step toward overcoming it. Then overcoming laziness requires

- awareness of why you've become lazy.
- determination.
- accountability to someone.
- a plan of action to change behavior.

Is overcoming laziness really all that important? Once you deal with your lethargy, you will find yourself moving far more quickly toward achieving your life mission. You'll probably soon realize you're making more money. And meaning will be restored to your life because you are living up to your true God-given potential.

Laziness in its purest form is self-destructive behavior. It actually leads to an entire lifestyle of self-destruction where every opportunity is blown and every challenge is missed.

Seven Costly Mistakes

Some of this stems from a shameful self-concept that doesn't feel worthy of success. It spills over into all relationships, none of which ever seem to be gratifying. If you are your own worst enemy, accepting your self-destructive nature is the beginning to changing it.

There are many lists of why people do not win and why they destroy their many opportunities to win. I believe that this list encompasses the traits of the losers I have known. If you find yourself struggling with winning, if you find yourself losing over and over again, review the list and examine your patterns of behavior. You can change. You can allow yourself to win. These seven costly mistakes do not have to plague your life. You can take control of becoming a winner at work and at home by becoming responsible in clarifying the mission of your life, learning to handle the money well, and comprehending the meaning of your life.

Summary:
Seven Costly Mistakes

1. The ultimate result of unbridled ambition is personal emptiness.
2. The person who manipulates people produces only temporary results.
3. Pride stands in the way of teamwork because it alienates rather than brings together.
4. Shameful incidents or passages of time may cause us to sabotage our positive accomplishments.
5. The fear of failure is far more detrimental to us in our careers than failure could ever be.
6. Avoid the pitfall of lust before you lose your balance and topple into it.
7. Laziness in its purest form is self-destructive behavior.

Part 2

The Mission

CHAPTER FOUR

In Search of a Mission

Winners don't usually win by accident. For every lottery winner, there are a thousand others who won because they lived their lives on purpose. There aren't a lot of people at the top who will tell you they "just kind of fell into" what they are doing. Now a few people may be tripped, but most don't stumble onto a great life mission. They might not have had their sights directly on their current work, but most of the time they found their life's work because they had a sense of mission and destiny.

Winners are looking for something. They aren't throwing their time and effort randomly at anything that comes along. There are goals to be set and met. There are hurdles to be jumped and obstacles to be removed. Successful people have in their minds what they want to do, how they are going to do it, and some idea of both the risks and the rewards of their

In Search of a Mission

efforts. If you want to succeed, it is a good idea to develop a mission that you can live with.

What is your mission in life? Have you thought about it? Have you taken all of your talents and experiences along with the desires of your heart and boiled them down into a concise understanding of the mission you are on? Would any friend or family member be able to accurately tell what mission you are on? Does anyone know your goals and how you are trying to accomplish them? Do you?

If you responded with a lot of noes, it is time that you lay the cornerstone to the foundation of everything you are doing professionally and personally. That cornerstone is a personal mission statement that reflects who you are, what you are doing, and the way in which you are doing it. You may be caught up in the momentum of earning a living, fulfilling your roles as a spouse and a parent, nurturing friendships, and meeting obligations without having a conscious awareness of where you're headed. You've never stopped to analyze what your life's purpose is all about. You function, do your best, and hope and pray that everything comes out all right.

A mission statement provides you with a compass. It states in black and white what you want to be, what you want to accomplish, and what your governing values are. It becomes both an anchor and a rudder. It is an anchor because it allows you to stay steadfastly in place while you decline offers and temptations that would distract you from your mission. It is a rudder because it helps you stay the course while you are moving toward your goals. A good mission statement can prevent a thousand failures and wasted effort. When you are confused by outside influences or internal emotional turmoil, the mission statement can be the solid rock that grounds your decisions in reality.

Before we go farther together, you need to be sure your mission statement is firmly in place in this book and in your mind. After that you will want to share it with your closest advisors so they can help you make future decisions based on the mission you have chosen.

I hope you will write in this book or keep a journal because if others come along years later and pick it up with your words in it, you will be benefiting them by allowing them to see who you really were. Additionally, when you write something down, it carries much more weight than if you just think it in your mind. So get started on developing a mission and a mission statement. If you already have one, this short exercise should help you revise and improve it.

This first question is probably the one that every college student should be forced to write about before graduation. It forces you to look at some of your fears that might be holding you back and where you might find yourself if you did not fear failure.

1. If you knew that you would succeed at whatever you attempted to do, and that the money would be there for you to do it, what would you do?

2. When you die, what would you like to have said about you and your accomplishments at your funeral?

3. Write a one-sentence epitaph for your tombstone. It should capsulate the key ingredients of your life.

4. What one skill have people told you over and over that you possess better than most other people? (It could be a manual skill in working with your hands or a perceptual skill in dealing with people.)

5. When you think of values and morals that you respect and attempt to apply to your life, which ones are the most impor-

In Search of a Mission

tant to you? (These could include things like honesty, perseverance, serving poor people, helping with a cause, giving back to God, leadership, or love.)

6. What have you done with your life so far that has brought you the most meaning? What are some things you hope to do in the future that promise to bring even more meaning?

7. When you think of your financial needs and goals, how much money will you need to accomplish what you want to accomplish, whether it is saving for retirement, putting your kids through college, or giving away a large sum to a cause or institution you support? (Develop a plan A that exceeds your expectations, a plan B that meets them, and a plan C that enables you to just get by.)

8. In what ways do you plan to spend the money you make? (Travel, savings, church, charity, retirement, education, luxury items, jewelry, cars, home, or investments?)

9. What one accomplishment could you complete that you feel would give you the most satisfaction and fulfillment?

10. Based on your education, experience, and feelings, and the comments of friends and family, what area of work do you think would most likely use your talents the best?

Before proceeding, look back at the words you have written and ponder their meaning. What might *you* be trying to tell yourself? (You might have been deceiving yourself because

you have been afraid of what the truth might demand of you.)
Is something within you trying to tell you something through
this exercise? Are you on the right path, or do you think you
are greatly underutilizing some of your distinctive gifts? After
taking time to consider these broad brush strokes of your life,
you are ready to engage in a more detailed process of goal
setting.

GOALS BEFORE GOLD

Writing a personal mission statement is, in a sense, the
ultimate goal-setting exercise. Actually, it is the distillation of
multiple goals into a central theme. If you haven't thought
concretely about the goals you can and would like to accomplish, now is the time to do it, especially before you compose
your first draft of a mission statement. When goals of a mission are balanced and healthy, they include family priorities,
not just business concerns. They incorporate values, not just
ambitions. Goals on the way to a mission involve relationships, not just productivity. They should take into account
your "ALOTment" factor. ALOT stands for

> *Assets*
> *Liabilities*
> Opportunities
> *Threats*

Each of us has a certain "ALOTment" of talents, weaknesses, opportunities, and challenges. These are the fibers of
our life missions and the goals we set. Some people plan to
conquer the world but seem unable to keep a job over a year.
They have no shortage of goals and plans, but they are without a realistic view of their limitations. Others are full of
strength and potential, yet they never realize all that is within
them. They end up sacrificing a life of greatness for nothing

more than an inferiority complex. Still others don't take into account their realistic opportunities. For example, if you want to be a Broadway star, it would help if you learned to sing and dance and lived near Broadway. You can't expect to get discovered sitting in Dalhart, Texas, if you want to be on Broadway. Consider your "ALOTment" before you develop your goals, and you will end up with some realistic goals that you will accomplish rather than merely hope to accomplish.

Some people balk at goal setting, even if the goal is a personal mission statement, for any number of reasons. Ted Engstrom, who is respected as a motivational speaker and author, cites a number of incentives for goal setting. Among those incentives are the following ones, which particularly apply to the goals expressed in defining a life's mission. The words in italic are Ted's (from his book *High Performance*); the other words are mine:

1. *Goals give a sense of direction and purpose.* A goal is like a lighthouse in your life. Even in the darkest, most turbulent times, you can see the way and know the destination. The biggest cause of floating aimlessly in a sea of confusion or crashing against the rocks of despair is the lack of a goal. Additionally, even if you fail, there is a sense of satisfaction in knowing that you were pursuing something beyond yourself, something worth the risk.

2. *Goals give us the power to live in the present.* If my goals for the future are clear, I have little trouble in prioritizing today. I know what I have to do today to be closer to the goal tomorrow. If I don't focus on what is essential today, I will be overcome with busyness and will do only what is urgent, not what moves me closer to the goal. The closer I get to the goal, the more present oriented I become.

3. *Goals promote enthusiasm.* There isn't much excite-

ment over bricklaying. It is rather mundane, requires some skill, but is repetitive and boring. If you ask me to lay bricks with you, I'm probably going to find something else to do. If you want me to get enthusiastic about bricklaying, invite me to be part of building a cathedral or a home for a homeless person. Now you have my attention and my enthusiasm. Goals do that for others and for me. If I have the finished product in mind, I am more likely to get excited about the parts I like doing the least.

4. *Goals help us operate more effectively.* I mentioned earlier the issue of busyness. It makes losers out of a lot of people. If you are busy, you can convince yourself you are doing a great job when you might just be killing time. A goal gives you a reason to do away with the things that are ineffective and focus on the things that are. If you know the goal, you can go after it and nothing else, like a French hog when truffles are in season. French hogs don't stop to cut their nails. They have a job to do, and they do it effectively.

5. *Goals help us to evaluate our progress.* Few things are as painful and as necessary as regular personal assessments. In any business the board or the bank will force you to evaluate and report where you are on the path to accomplishing the corporate goals. You need to do the same for yourself by taking each individual goal and seeing if over the past three months you came closer to it or moved farther away from it. The reality of that evaluation is the key to making the best decisions on how to further your mission. It is done by discovering that you are behind or ahead one goal at a time.

6. *Goals force us to plan ahead.* If I am aware of where I want to end up, I am more likely to stop and think of what I am going to need to get there. If I want to be a

psychologist, doing that will be quite hard without a Ph.D. Knowing my goal, I can determine the education or the experience or other resources I must amass to make it happen. Without planning I will always feel behind and unprepared. Being secure in my goals and the direction I want my life to take forces me to plan and helps me enjoy the task. Planning is delayed gratification in action. An ounce of planning usually results in a pound of accomplishment.

7. *Goals help us to communicate.* One of the things I learned early in business is that everyone thinks everybody else knows exactly what he or she is talking about. The ability to communicate is far less than perceived by the one doing the communicating. The fact is, people need to be shown the big picture. They need to see a picture of the end result. Goals provide that picture and a common point of reference when assessing performance, motivating people to produce, or asking for assistance in overcoming an obstacle. If you are unclear about your goals, you will have a hard time communicating with those who are needed to help you accomplish the goals.

8. *Goals give us a clear understanding of what is expected.* Goals are great gifts in any business or personal relationship. If I am involved with you personally and ask you to help me help others, you might think that noble and sign on. A different reaction might come from knowing I wanted to help people in the jungles of Papua, New Guinea, where the infant mortality rate in some tribes is 100 percent for as long as seven years at a time. Helping people in the United States requires compassion and knowledge. Helping people in New Guinea requires training in jungle survival. Every goal unlocks a door to realistic expectations so that accurate decisions can be made about the

worthiness of a goal and the effort required to achieve it.

   With goals having all that going for them, you would think that most people would walk around with a mighty fine updated list of them. Sadly, most people don't ever think of a goal other than that they want to be rich or famous. There is no time like now to develop a set of realistic goals, based on a realistic assessment of your "ALOTment." Once you have completed this next section, you will be ready to write your mission statement with depth.

Goal-Setting Exercise of_____

1. List three goals that you want to accomplish before you die.

2. What strengths and resources do you possess that could help you accomplish them?

3. What are some weaknesses and questions that will need to be resolved if you are to achieve these goals?

4. What doors have opened up for you that would indicate you have a chance at achieving these goals?

5. What are the three biggest roadblocks that you will have to overcome in order to succeed?

6. What is the unifying theme of your three goals that indicates they are all part of the same mission?

7. What is the one thing that will bring you the greatest disappointment if you don't accomplish it?

8. List five goals you set for yourself in the past that you have succeeded in accomplishing.

RELATIONSHIPS AND THE REALIZATION OF GOALS

Starting out on a mission, many end up on something more like a missile, pointed toward the goal but flying alone. They don't start out that way, but pressures and egos start to build. They end up like the following couple who had great intentions but were a little weak on follow-through. It is a common story that has been the ruin of many bright and talented people. Whether you are single or married, this story could save you some pain if you learn from their experiences.

David owned a busy recording studio. Sheila, his wife, had chosen to stay home and take care of their four small children. David and Sheila loved each other very much. Before the children came along, she worked with him in building up his business. She managed his office for years, while he worked as an engineer on record projects. After their first child was born, they made the decision that a hired employee would replace Sheila, and she would devote the next few years to mothering.

All that was done with the best of intentions. And at first, the communication lines remained open. Sheila was genuinely interested in the studio's clients and ongoing projects, and of course, David loved his children dearly. However, as months and years passed, Sheila began to focus all her attention on the kids—the daily frustrations, first steps, new words, tantrums, and runny noses. Meanwhile her husband, distracted by challenges and concerns at work, found his mind wandering as she told him story after story about their little ones.

He became inattentive.

She became resentful: "He never talks to me when he comes home. And he doesn't listen when I talk to him."

Some people call it compartmentalizing. Others call it splitting off. Wives think of it as being "shut out." Husbands classify it under "I'll never understand women." Whatever it's called, a very familiar and uncomfortable situation arises between significant others when work life and home life aren't permitted to mix.

In marriages where men earn the money, men are often accused of living for their jobs. And a woman frequently builds her world around her husband, only to find that he has focused his attention totally on his career. Or she builds her life around her children, only to have them rebel. Eventually, they move out and on with their lives, leaving her empty and wanting something more out of life. There are always exceptions to this pattern, and the roles may be reversed. However, everyone knows about the man who just "isn't here for me when he gets home." And we've also heard more often than we care to repeat the tale of the wife who "just doesn't understand me or my life."

These situations sometimes start out very early in a marriage when a way of life is being established. Young couples are often uninformed about the mistakes they may be making, foolishly assuming that love conquers all. In other cases, as with David and Sheila, the problem arises later, after children come along and priorities change. In any case, the problem of drifting apart can be prevented—or turned around—through determination and communication.

Naturally, that communication is best established at the beginning, when your life's mission is still being formed. There is nothing more important than, at the outset of both marriage and career, for a husband and a wife to sit down and

In Search of a Mission

talk about the future. When a mission statement for either spouse is developed, both spouses should be part of the decision-making process. The wording should be agreed upon. The family's values, financial concerns, and priorities should be discussed and debated calmly over a period of time. Does the husband intend to work outside the home or in a home office? Does the wife want to stay home for a few years or develop a parallel career from the outset? What about children? What about aging parents? Some specific questions should be asked regarding the role of each spouse.

If you are married or about to be married, sit down with the person you love, and write out the answers to the following questions together.

Where should we live?

How far should each of us commute?

Are we willing to move?

When do we plan to start a family?

How much money do we need to save for the time when I'll be staying home and taking care of the children?

How far should I try to advance? What is the highest position I should try to reach?

What kind of salary goals should we set for our family?

What's the least we can live on?

What salary level will rob our family of time together?

How many hours per week will I spend at work in order to meet our family's goals regarding position and salary?

What kind of sacrifices are we willing to make in order for me to achieve salary and position goals?

What kind of retirement income will we need? How do we plan to attain it?

What vacation and relaxation time are we willing to give up in order to meet our goals?

When a husband and a wife work as a team to meet career and family goals, twice as much energy is focused on meeting the goals. In essence, this doubles the power of each spouse. Anyone who has been in a marriage where they were attempting to achieve exactly the opposite goals knows that the marriage can put you in an institution. The anger, frustration, and disappointment from two people going opposite directions are unbearable. Just imagine how many marriages could have been saved or never started if people had reviewed all these issues before the knot was tied.

If you are already married and well on your way to achieving your goals and accomplishing your mission, you might want to take a minute or two to evaluate how well you are doing in the area of personal partnership. Here are ten questions to ask yourself as you think about how well you are doing at including your loved ones in your life's mission:

1. Have I had dinner with my family more than once in the past week?
2. What did I talk to my spouse about over the past few days?
3. Do I have any secrets I can't share with my spouse? Am I "protecting" my spouse from potentially disturbing information?
4. Am I more comfortable discussing business with my assistant or another coworker than with my spouse?
5. Am I bored with the conversations at home?
6. Do I detect resentment from my spouse when certain people's names arise in conversation?
7. Am I giving equal conversation time to my spouse's interests as to my own?
8. How do I feel about taking my spouse to office parties, picnics, or other social events?
9. Have I taken more than one week of vacation in the past year?
10. Do I give as much attention to managing family finances as I do to succeeding at business projects?

A "no" answer to any of these questions could be an indication of a problem that has been stewing or perhaps is just brewing. Sit down and talk with your spouse about how it's going so far. Seek an objective professional if you need help to communicate.

WRITING THE MISSION STATEMENT

Once you have spent time considering all these issues, you are ready to write a mission statement. Let me use my mission statement as an example for you writing yours:

WINNING AT WORK

Mission Statement of Stephen Arterburn

I would like to lead an organization in helping people with addictions and emotional problems find a new way to live, turning their lives over to God rather than attempting to run them and thus ruin them alone. I want to continue to improve my skills as a writer and speaker, increasing the percentage of my income earned in those endeavors. In doing that I would like to make enough money to allow my daughter to go to college and my wife and I to have the freedom to do missionary projects around the world when we retire. While accomplishing these goals I want to become wise in God's Word and expand my hobbies of music, painting, and scuba diving. Throughout my life I hope to attract wise and wonderful friends that grow closer as I grow older. Everything I do, I will do to build the love I have for my family and the love they have for me. In the end, I will work so that my life can be characterized by the following six words: *generosity, compassion, creativity, perseverance, wisdom,* and *integrity.*

There it is. It reflects my goals and my heart. If I stay true to this statement, I will be able to have the fulfillment that I long for. When I am tempted to leave the frustrating field I am in, I come back to this mission, and I realize that no amount of money in another field of work would satisfy me like seeing lives changed. Before we get back to your composing your own mission statement, let me digress into why my work must be involved with helping people.

One night a man was driving in his car with tremendous desperation in his heart. He was having a combination of homicidal and suicidal thoughts. The pressures of his life were too great, and he feared that he might end the lives of his family and then take his own. When he was younger, he had attended a Christian rock concert, and at the end of that night he committed his life to God. His long-lost dream had been to become a Christian rock musician like the one who had led him down the aisle to Jesus. Those dreams were faded into impossibility. As he considered his worthless life, he begged God to help him. He pleaded for God to break through time and space and reach into his life and help him with his struggles.

As one last act of faith, he told God that he would turn on the radio, and he asked God to help him through giving him a resource to call. When he turned on the radio, he heard my voice doing a spot for our treatment centers offering hope by calling 1-800-NEW-LIFE. He had a car phone and called the number and talked to an intake worker. With a few words he made the decision to drive directly to the center, and he was admitted that night.

While he was going through the admission process, he told the admissions counselor the story of making a commitment at a Christian rock concert years ago, but the hopes he had then had turned to nothing but disappointment. As he told the story of the Christian musician, the admissions counselor's eyes lit up. He knew God had an incredible surprise in store for this desperate man.

When the papers were completed, the admissions counselor walked him back to the unit. A man saw him enter the unit and walked up the hall directly to him and introduced himself. After telling him his name, he told the new patient that everyone on the unit had to have a buddy and he asked this young man to be his. The new patient could hardly believe his eyes. You see, his new friend was actually an old one. It was the Christian rock star, no longer on a stage, but seeking help for himself and his own problems.

Before they both left treatment, they gave a joint concert for the patients, and I was privileged to attend it. This is just one of a thousand stories I know of hope and restoration and of God using our efforts to help others. As long as these events continue to make my heart roar with joy, I will continue my mission of helping others.

My desire for you would be to think beyond the pay-check and the possibility of retirement and consider what you could do that would add the most fulfillment to your life and the lives of your family. How could you have an influence on people who could use your talents and strengths? When you consider these things, you are actually determining what kind of person you want to be. You consider what principles you will respect. There is a move away from totally focusing on what you will accomplish to more of an analysis of how best you can contribute.

Having a mission statement is not a means to an end, only the beginning of a lifelong process. And since we humans are somewhat mistake prone, we need to consider up front some of the things that can go wrong with the creation of mission statements as well as with the process of trying to fulfill them.

If my mission statement didn't help you clarify the ele-ments to place in yours, perhaps this example will be more helpful:

Mission Statement of Kevin Jenkins

I, Kevin Jenkins, want to be a highly respected real estate agent in my community, as well as a loving husband and father, and a loyal friend. I will provide for my family financially as generously as I possibly can. I want to be a real estate counselor who offers guidance to people who are making one of the most important decisions of their lives. I hope to write at least one book that expresses my perspective, and to get it published. I also wish to lecture, present seminars, and eventually have my own agency. I will work under the authority of my personal religious faith and its guidelines such as the golden rule and the Ten Commandments. I will not sacrifice integrity for success.

I'd sure like to buy a house from Kevin Jenkins. It makes me wonder how many sincere and dedicated people we would want to do business with if we knew the mission they were on instead of assuming they were only out to make money or, worse yet, rip us off.

Words, especially written ones, have power. Writing a mission statement does not guarantee compliance with it, but the act of writing it out is almost like making a commitment to yourself and others. When you have composed yours, I think you will be surprised at just how much power is there to help you make good, solid decisions about today that will lead you to the tomorrows of your dreams.

Dreams are accomplished by balanced people on a worthwhile mission with the skills and resources necessary to accomplish the mission. I've noted some cautions in writing a mission statement to ensure that the dreams aren't dashed before they are ever firmly rooted in place:

- Mission Caution #1: Some individuals separate the corporate mission statement from the personal mission statement. Then they fail to recognize the toll the corporate mission is taking on their private lives. This is a dangerous mistake. When only corporate, business, or even humanitarian goals become a person's priority, family and friends get left in the dust. When friends and family aren't included in your mission statement, they will most likely be ignored in daily living, too.

- Mission Caution #2: By becoming overfocused on one part of the mission statement, you may fail to meet your other equally important goals. For example, Kevin Jenkins, the fictitious real estate agent in the sample mission statement, might become obsessed with the idea of writing a book at the expense of his need to get out there and show people houses. Or in an attempt to make a place for himself by owning his own agency, he could ignore his religious values and become a cutthroat competitor.

- Mission Caution #3: Setting unrealistic goals can cause discouragement and disappointment. Either overestimating your capabilities or undervaluing your talent can create a mission statement that is too hard to live up to or too easy to fulfill. Either way, you're likely to lose your focus.

- Mission Caution #4: When you fail to reassess your mission from time to time, you find yourself out of touch with present reality. For instance, when the children grow up and move out, part of the vision statement has to be redrawn. When you reach a higher level of achievement, you may need to set higher goals. Reassessment and adjustment are necessary from time to time.

- Mission Caution #5: Attaching personal worth, meaning, and identity to your mission promises an eventual personal crisis. Although your mission statement should reflect your value, meaning, and identity, accomplishing your mission cannot provide these things. You have to find them elsewhere. In other words, your mission statement should be meaningful to you, but you must always acknowledge that the true mission and meaning of your life come from the Creator of your life.

- Mission Caution #6: Sometimes you believe one way and act another. You may be mentally committed to your mission, but in practical terms you aren't really living out what you say you believe in. It's important to keep an eye on your actions so that you aren't being hypocritical with yourself. Consistency of action, congruency between thought and action, and perseverance are key ingredients to seeing a mission through and finding fulfillment.
- Mission Caution #7: People who stand for nothing believe in nothing, fight for nothing, fall for anything, and eventually fall for something that amounts to nothing. You may not be the greatest mission statement writer, but an incomplete mission statement is better than none. If you do nothing else, take the time to nail down the three most important things in your life that you would stand up for, fight for, and perhaps even die for.

It's time to write your mission statement. I hope you have taken the time to write out the exercises because your writing here will be easier and more meaningful. Consider first what it is that makes your heart roar with joy. Be sure that is at the heart of your mission statement. Look back at mine and look at Mr. Jenkins's for the elements you want to include as you craft your own. Go back over the written workbook section to find those things you wrote that really mean something to you. Your first draft doesn't have to be wonderful. It is just a starting point that you can revise and improve on over the years to come.

The Mission Statement of

WINNING AT WORK

You have just completed a very important beginning. It is the right place to begin the journey of winning and finding fulfillment in work and love. We are all on a mission, and we are all fulfilling one. Some are misguided, and some are confused. Nonetheless, the mission of every individual is in place. What a sense of accomplishment to have a mission statement to come back to and see that you are indeed farther along the course that you have charted for yourself. Or better yet, to discover that some job, relationship, or deal has gotten you off track, and through evaluation, you make the tough decisions to bring your life back in line with what you had planned and what you believe God would want for your life.

If you aren't married but you are thinking about getting married, be sure you share your mission statement with your future spouse. And don't forget to ask that future mate about his or her mission statement. A lot of pain and heartache can be saved when people openly and honestly admit that they love each other, but they are on two entirely different tracks toward fulfillment.

If you are married, I think your spouse will be delighted to hear that you have worked this out and that it includes the family. A healthy exercise would be for you to use your statement as an example and ask each person in your family to develop one.

Now that you have a mission statement and a clearer view of where you would like your time and effort to take you, it is time to consider the way you will get there. Leadership will drive your mission if it is to be a successful one. It is up to you to lead, and in the next chapter you will find ways to develop the skills and attitudes of a leader.

Summary:
Seven Mission Cautions

1. Some individuals separate the corporate mission statement from the personal mission statement.
2. By becoming overfocused on one part of the mission statement, you may fail to meet your other equally important goals.
3. Setting unrealistic goals can cause discouragement and disappointment.
4. When you fail to reassess your mission from time to time, you may find yourself out of touch with present reality.
5. Attaching personal worth, meaning, and identity to your mission promises an eventual personal crisis.
6. Sometimes you believe one way and act another.
7. People who stand for nothing believe in nothing, fight for nothing, fall for anything, and eventually fall for something that amounts to nothing.

CHAPTER FIVE

Leadership

Everybody knows about the henpecked, subservient husband who is a tyrant at the office. We've all seen the charming salesman who is dearly loved by all his customers (especially the women) but is despised by his verbally abused wife. We've watched the successful pastor whose children are in trouble with the law. And we've seen the unemployed husband who doesn't have time to look for a job but takes the baby to the park every day. In each of these examples there is a lack of balance and follow-through, an inconsistency that leads to failure.

Is it possible to be a strong leader both at home and at work? Yes. But not without a conscious decision to have the best of both worlds. And not without an understanding that mission, money, and meaning have to be balanced for our personal and professional lives to blend together. Leadership begins with concern about those for whom we have responsibility. In fact, we practice the best leadership when we meet the needs of others. When we apply the golden rule to leadership, we remove the element of authoritarianism, and we replace it with mutual concern: I care about you just as much as I care about myself. This attitude is invaluable at work. And it is irreplaceable at home. Dwight D. Eisenhower once said, "You do not lead by hitting people over the head—that's assault, not leadership." I heartily agree.

This servant-leader attitude is not something found in viewing film clips of tyrant leaders such as Adolf Hitler. It is also rare to see examples of it in the presidents' offices of major corporations. It is there, but it is seldom seen. Fortunately, the trend is going in the right direction, and we are seeing more and more examples of this true leadership, void of manipulation or dictatorial rule. I am sure that if you want to lead an organization to success in the nineties and on into the next century, you will have to adjust your view of leadership away from authoritarianism and to a servant-leader model.

ELEMENTS OF LEADERSHIP

Having run a successful operation with dedicated board members and a marvelous team of people, I have come to know many fine leaders who shared some common characteristics. I have listed some of these characteristics below. The one common element that I have seen in the leaders I have known is that when they left work, they took their leadership skills with them. Think about these ten leadership skills that can apply both at home and at work.

1. Have Commitment

People with commitment can usually be spotted with a quick review of their resumes. Anyone who has had ten jobs in ten years may have a lot of things, but commitment most likely isn't one of them. People with this essential quality stay, even during the tough times. Recently, I was meeting with a man whose treatment center was being merged with our operations. He had started the center and made it the success it was when I met him. Upon interviewing him, I discovered a trait that probably resulted in some of the difficulties that had begun to emerge in the center. The man stated to me that as long as the place made money, he would be there. The minute it began to lose, he would be gone. I told him how surprised I was, since he would be the most logical one to help the center make changes if it ran into difficulties. He said that wasn't in his blood. He was the kind of person who helped something get bigger, not smaller.

You can see the difficulty this attitude presents. It is an adult way of saying that if things don't go just like I want them, I will take my toys and play with someone else. Companies need people who will persevere through the bad times so that the companies will be around to enjoy the good times. If you want to lead, have the attitude of "I'm not going to bail out of this if it gets difficult. I'm here to stay—to work through the tough times and to celebrate the good times." That kind of attitude gets attention, and it motivates others to follow you.

It is easy to see the parallel value to a business and a marriage or a relationship when a person is able to make and keep a commitment. The person with the lengthy resume from too many job changes probably will have a few marriages in the past, also. Either that or no marriages because when a difficulty pops up, the noncommitted pop out of the relationship. Leaders commit, even when and especially when it doesn't feel good to stay in a commitment. That really is what commitment is all about: acting and leading even when it is painful.

2. Share Profits

When I started my company in 1988, I made it clear to the board of directors that I wanted every employee to be a part owner by granting everyone stock options in the company. With that plan implemented, when the company does well, everyone does well. Our people aren't working to make me more successful—they're working to make us more successful in every way. We are all in this together.

If you have been blessed with success, be sure that people see you lead by generously sharing some of what you produce with others in the organization or people less fortunate than yourself. A greedy miser has few friends and ends up with fewer opportunities for advancement. If the thought of sharing what you earn with others makes you a bit nauseous, you might want to get some help in holding on to what God has given you a little more loosely.

3. Motivate Partners

People don't lead to the top alone. You can't be a leader if you have no followers. Real leaders want to do well, but they want to see a lot of others do well, also. Communicate to coworkers and people you supervise that you want to see them fulfill their potential as persons. Encourage them and assist them in building their self-confidence in every way. The more people you attract to your team, the more likely you will succeed. Beating people down only drives away the real winners and destroys those who could become winners.

There was a time when many people thought there were two major motivators in business. The positive one was money, and the negative one was fear. Most successful people no longer believe in the old theory. Of course, money still motivates, and fear keeps people moving, but if you want all you can get out of a person, it takes more. You must show appreciation for a job well done and encouragement when things do not go according to plan. Being appreciative is usually easy to do when the results are there; offering encouragement when times are tough seems to be much harder. Leaders find a way to give their people what they need when they need it. Money, support, and appreciation are all part of the motivation equation.

4. Communicate with Partners

Following along the lines of how to motivate people, we must never underestimate the power of information. People want it, and if they don't receive it, they always perform far below their potential. No matter how bad the news, anyone being brought into the information loop will have a 50 percent better chance of rising to the occasion than someone who has been left out. Hard as it may seem, leaders are always trying to find new ways to share as much information as possible with people.

Communication leads to understanding the task at hand and the key personnel who must work together to achieve the task. If you want to gather around you a team of champions, dedicated to accomplishing great things, be sure they understand you and your motivation before you involve them with the work. Pledge to the people who work with you that you will let them know your expectations, and vow to never use silence as negative reinforcement or withhold information as a way of manipulating.

If you are a follower rather than a leader, you can get ahead by becoming an accurate source of information. People at the top are often shut out from how things really are at the bottom or the middle. Never withhold information that could be vital in your supervisor's decision making. Your greatest chance for advancement is to become known as someone who sees what is taking place and works to fix the problems as they arise.

5. Show Appreciation

Don't just applaud success; reward it. Use everything from money to parties to trips to show that you appreciate a job well done. Most leaders take time to create. Creating ways to highlight accomplishments shows you are more interested in rewarding the performance of your people instead of trying primarily to meet your own needs.

If you can learn to motivate people at work, you have the same ability to be the greatest motivator at home—through the fine art of encouragement. Encouragement begins when you step outside yourself and see other people's need to be appreciated. A good place to begin, of course, is with your spouse. Your children. Your parents. Your in-laws. In fact, it's far more difficult to be an encourager at home. When you live under the same roof with people, you know them too well, and the positive words may not flow so freely.

6. Search for Successes

Leaders never stop looking for others who would make a valuable contribution to the team. In all your networking outside your organization, always keep an eye or an ear open for potential winners to add to your team. It could make a radical difference in your success.

The person I rely on the most is a young man named Burt Wilson. He is by far the brightest and most talented individual I have ever worked with. I found him working in my father-in-law's company. I knew I had a greater need and a greater opportunity so I went after him and he joined our organization. He essentially is in control of every area of the organization, allowing me to focus on marketing and financing the company. Whether it is a winner to work for you or with you, never stop searching for someone with talent and leadership potential.

7. Listen to Others' Opinions

Others have valuable ideas that would never come to you. Even when others have weak ideas, it helps to listen to them, analyze why they don't work, and develop some of your own from their weak ones. One of the surest signs of leadership gone awry is an ego so big that no one's opinion counts except that of the leader. Everyone can make a contribution if you are willing to listen. Great leaders find a way to cultivate the minds of others to form the great ideas that lead to success.

8. Exceed Expectations

In my company each person goes through an orientation process with me. It takes a while to get everyone through it, but I eventually orient everyone. When I am with a group of new employees, the message that I think is most valuable is this one: "Be a bargain to the company." Whether people are earning $20,000 or $200,000, they will be considered a bargain and have job security if they will exceed expectations. The comment people want uttered about them is, "That's the last person I would want to leave the company." The only way to instill that attitude in others about you is to be sure you are always performing above expectations.

Obviously, if you don't know a person's expectations of you, you will fail at meeting them. So ask. And ask how you are doing. If the expectations are unrealistic and cannot be made more realistic, as painful as it may be, you will have learned that you can never exceed expectations, and you must move on to a job where you can exceed expectations.

9. Control Expenses

Anyone can do almost anything with unlimited resources. The leader finds a way to do great things with limited resources. The more you can do with the less money, the greater your success and the more will be entrusted to you. There is always a temptation to play the role of the big spender. Money brings power, and when you spend it, it makes you feel powerful. But that source of power is fleeting. For example, if you walked into a department store and put $5,000 down on the counter and said you wanted to buy some clothes, you would instantly become the most powerful person in that store. People would do anything they could to make you feel good and spend your money. But when you walk out, your power stays in the store. You foolishly gave it away.

Real monetary power does not come from spending; it comes from saving, whether it is the company's money or your own. Keeping money brings the greatest rewards. Since the financial attitude at the top is caught by all people throughout the organization, leaders knowingly show restraint in their spending.

10. Don't Be Afraid to Be Original

Creativity is the most rewarding aspect of any project or endeavor. If we allow our imaginations to be free, anything is possible! Successful people take time to be successful. They take time to create. They never get so busy that they don't have time for solitude when their activity is minimal and their creativity is maximized.

I don't believe that people either are born with leadership skills or are born without them. I believe the skills can be developed and nurtured. Don't just accept that nothing can be done to improve your ability to lead. You can make a decision to be a leader and develop what skills you have into much greater opportunity. Leadership takes hard work; any kind of responsibility does. Anything you can do to advance yourself as a leader will provide you and those who work with you with great rewards.

As you take a leadership role, you find very soon that it's

not something you can fake—you have to do it. People who are looking up to you will see through you very quickly if you aren't making a wholehearted effort to encourage them, be a good example, and set a standard for excellence. To those whom much is given much more is expected. Always work to be worthy of the opportunities that have come your way.

The opportunity to lead is a gift. Did it ever occur to you that your leadership roles, both at work and at home, are divine appointments for you? If you believe, as I do, that God has a plan for each of our lives, you can see your leadership responsibilities in a new light. Maybe ministers aren't the only ones on a mission from God. Your gift from God is an opportunity to motivate people to take limited resources and create something of value that was not there before. Looking at leadership from that perspective, you come to realize that being a leader is a divine honor.

FARTHER ALONG THE LEADERSHIP TRAIL

Whether the mission is being acted out at home or at the office, there are some additional principles to meeting goals every leader needs to know—and use wisely. They will help you stay on track; they will also help you inspire and encourage your spouse as well as the rest of your family. Consider each of these five leadership tasks that leaders must tend to every day.

1. Keep Communication Open

You can make the difference both at home and at work by how you relate and communicate. Naturally, the communication channels sometimes get clogged up. Communication wipeouts include the following:

- Insensitivity
- Preoccupation
- Panic
- Indecisiveness
- Impatience
- Insecurity
- Anger
- Fear of confrontation

All of these problems that stand in the way of good communication are part of every relationship from time to time. You will not be able to avoid them 100 percent. The leader knows they will arise, and the leader determines that when they do, it is the leader's role to fix them, to reopen the downed communication lines.

2. Know Where You Are, Where You Are Going, and Why

As a leader, you are being looked to for direction. You may get so busy that you forget where you are and the direction you need to give to accomplish your plan. Be the one who always has a way of figuring out what the next few steps are, especially when all is not going exactly according to plan. Be ready to recite the purpose of the mission because the people you lead will always question your motives. Whether generals in battle or astronauts thousands of miles out in space, leaders know where they are, where they are going, and why.

3. Continue to Evaluate What You Are Up Against

When a problem arises, it may not be what you first think. To put it in medical terms, you could be dealing with a symptom rather than the sickness itself. Make sure your diagnosis is accurate. Then begin the problem-solving process a step at a time.

If you're honest with yourself, you may be up against

your own attitude. Every day we win or lose, not because of the battle out there, but because of the battle inside our souls. And as Napoleon once said, "The most dangerous moment comes with victory."

Attitude is everything (at least it is for a leader).

4. When a Mistake Is Made, Get Over It and Get On with It

Avoid stubbornness, and change your course rather than give up completely. Here are some interesting facts to think about when you've made a mistake and you're feeling like throwing in the towel:

- Great quarterbacks complete only six out of ten passes.
- Top oil companies find oil only one out of ten times they drill.
- Stock market winners win only two out of five times.
- Actors get turned down twenty out of thirty times before they sign for one commercial.

The biggest issue isn't problems, failures, or setbacks. The biggest concern is what you do with your problems. Common responses include abusing alcohol and/or drugs, overeating, having affairs, or becoming depressed. However, the best possible resolution is to try and try again. As Winston Churchill said,

*Never, never,
never, never,
never give up!*

Leaders, if they do nothing else, persevere.

5. Recognize That Who You Are Is Less Important Than What You Are Willing to Do

The most important thing about getting somewhere with your God, your life, your job, and your family is to start where you are. If you have a title or were born into a wealthy family with a famous reputation, forget about those things. They are merely platforms from which you can perform and have a more significant impact on the world. Who wants to have a great title but be considered of little value to anyone? Take how you are, and use it to do gracious things for other people.

We make a living by what we get. We make a life by what we give. Leaders have a greater opportunity than followers to win and give more. No matter what kind of leader you have been in the past, you can decide to be a new and different leader, a better leader tomorrow. Leaders are made, not born. If you don't have anyone making you into a leader, go to work on yourself. Decide that your model will be the servant leader who looks out for others first and gets ahead when others get ahead, also. Take on that attitude toward leadership and you will find the fulfillment you are looking for.

Summary:
Ten Elements of Leadership

1. Have commitment.
2. Share profits.
3. Motivate partners.
4. Communicate with partners.
5. Show appreciation.
6. Search for successes.
7. Listen to others' opinions.
8. Exceed expectations.
9. Control expenses.
10. Don't be afraid to be original.

Five Leadership Tasks

1. Keep communication open.
2. Know where you are, where you are going, and why.
3. Continue to evaluate what you are up against.
4. When a mistake is made, get over it and get on with it.
5. Recognize that who you are is less important than what you are willing to do.

CHAPTER SIX

Surround Yourself with Winners

If you are going to be able to fulfill your life mission, you must surround yourself with winners. Whether you are at home or in the workplace, cooperation and teamwork are necessary to succeed. It is far easier to succeed when people you depend on to work with you are not working against you (and themselves—as losers sometimes do).

Talented people are hard to find and often even harder to keep. We may not always hire the most talented individuals because they pose a threat to our security. We fear they may get ahead. I want to challenge your thinking. I want to invite you to look for people who could threaten your job. I want you to look for people who might get ahead of you and drag you along behind them. It is a different way of doing business and attracting personnel, and it is rarely ever done.

When I have learned about the operations of some organizations that have problems, I have been amazed at the incompetent people hired by top management. Out of insecurity and the need to control everything, they attract a wide variety of people who know how to say only one thing: Yes! Problems go unsolved, and the organization never reaches its full potential because of the disabled society that is formed at the top. I don't know this only from organizations I have seen at a distance; some of the organizations I have created have been plagued by the same problem. Though it has been difficult, I have been able to restructure the organization, replacing incompetence with aggressive talent.

Right now as I am writing this book, my organization is in the hands of Burt Wilson, who is twice as bright as I am and ten years younger. I am committed to his taking my place. I am committed to helping him learn everything he can so that he won't have to make the same mistakes I made. When he succeeds—and I know that he will—I will have some satisfaction in knowing that I helped him get there. Right alongside Burt is a very talented woman, Pam Van Dyke, who works in the operation of our centers. She knows my heart and carries out every task as if I were doing it, except that she does it better. Sharon Barnes, a former secretary of mine, now runs our most profitable operation. These are the kinds of people you must surround yourself with to succeed and meet your full potential.

Your motto needs to become this: hire over my head, and when I don't, let the people go quickly so they can move on to another job where they can succeed and others around them will be able to succeed, also. As I have learned the hard way, keeping an unsuccessful employee in the organization is too big a struggle with too big a price to pay for much too little return and much too much misery.

I want to tell you the story of Gordon, who fell into the emotional trap that often comes when we hire poorly and fire slowly.

Surround Yourself with Winners

Gordon was a self-made man in his early fifties, and he was proud of his accomplishments. He owned more than a dozen major commercial buildings in the Orange County area, and he enjoyed the challenge of managing them. He had found a comfortable social circle for himself at the yacht club, and his life was orderly, if somewhat lonely. A rough childhood with a distant father and a smothering, overwhelming mother left him without the skills to develop and nurture a long-term relationship.

When Marge, his longtime assistant, retired, Gordon was rather relieved. She had gotten a little too close, and her prying questions about his life made him more and more uneasy. It seemed that every day she worked there, she came to resemble his mother more and more. Even though she was excellent at what she did, she didn't have a chance at a long work relationship with Gordon as long as she resembled his unpleasant parent with whom he had never resolved his childhood resentment. When Maria came in for an interview in response to his classified ad for an office manager, Gordon felt an immediate sense of enthusiasm.

Besides being quite attractive and engaging, Maria had a fairly impressive resume. She had managed other offices, and it appeared that she worked well on her own. But Gordon really liked her personality—she had a sort of winsome quality that seemed almost, well, helpless. Gordon felt immediately attracted to her and somehow protective of her.

Maria was a single mother with two difficult teenagers, and her situation at home caused her to be late for work a couple of times during her first week of employment. Gordon was mildly annoyed, but a lunchtime conversation with Maria reminded him that it wasn't easy getting high-school students out of the house in the morning. He voiced his sympathy— one of his children had gone through a rebellious period, too. Maria seemed a little sad as they talked, and Gordon's heart went out to her.

WINNING AT WORK

After a couple more weeks on the job, Maria began to get calls from creditors. She explained she had cosigned for an ex-boyfriend, who was now in jail. Gordon wondered how such a nice woman could be tangled up with a loser like that, but he didn't comment. He did notice, however, that the ledger wasn't up to date when he looked at it, and the checkbooks hadn't been balanced in several days. When he pointed this out to Maria, she teared up. "I . . . I've had a lot on my mind," she said softly. "I'm so sorry." (If this scenario is starting to sound familiar, you are definitely reading the right chapter. You are not alone.)

Weeks went by, and as each one passed, more tasks remained unfinished or were improperly completed. Gordon, who was rather infatuated with Maria, was also experiencing a sinking feeling when he thought about his professional operation. Meanwhile, Maria had been evicted from her apartment, and Gordon had hurriedly helped her find another one. Her landlady had been terribly unreasonable with Maria, which troubled Gordon. He felt the poor young woman had been victimized, and he couldn't see why she'd had such a string of bad luck.

By the time he and I talked, his bookkeeping system was in complete disarray, several legal documents hadn't been filed at the proper time, causing serious repercussions, and he was in the process of covering a dozen bounced checks—all because of Maria's "distraction."

"She's such a sweetheart," he began, shaking his head. "I just hate to add to her troubles by complaining all the time."

I looked my friend in the eye, and as kindly as possible, I said, "I think you'd better fire her before it's too late."

"Fire her?" His eyes widened. He looked at me as if I'd told him to shoot Maria. "FIRE her?"

"You can be her friend if you want," I told him, "but I have this philosophy of management I think you'd better consider very carefully. It goes like this: the sooner you release an unsuccessful person to find a new place to be successful, the sooner you will find someone to help you succeed. It makes sense, doesn't it?"

So why don't we do it? Sometimes out of weakness, sometimes out of guilt, and sometimes out of ego, we decide that we can succeed in business, and we can fix people. Just their association with us can become a healing salve that can change behavior patterns that have built up for years.

It won't work. Act to surround yourself with winners, and the only way to do that is to occasionally eliminate someone who is not using talent and skills to win alongside you and help you win.

QUALITIES OF A WINNER

There are some qualities that make people winners. It isn't that hard to size up people based on these qualities. It takes some time and effort, but you can do it. I guess you could call this my top ten list to hiring winners.

1. Honesty

Of course, this is obvious, but it is rare to find. If you run an organization, people you supervise may tend to distort the truth to meet some of their own needs. They may also try to distort the picture you have of them in order to secure their jobs. It is rare to find someone with the courage to be honest. If you do, you should never discourage that person by not acting on the honest presentation of truth.

If you want to know the degree of honesty you can count on when hiring a person, make a thorough check of that person's resume. See if there is congruency between what you were told and what others tell you about the person. Once I was in search of a marketing person, and I found a man. The guy knew how to market, and they hated to lose him from the organization. We were hiring him based on his reputation with them and his outgoing personality.

On the man's resume was the mention of a college from a town back East. I called to verify that he had attended the school and had obtained the degree he stated. He didn't need the degree; I just wanted to verify that I was dealing with an honest individual. I was not. First of all, the school turned out to be a junior college that did not give out bachelor's degrees. Second, the school had no record that he had ever been there. I called him and withdrew my offer based on the dishonest representation on the resume. Before I hung up with him, I explained that the degree didn't matter, and I urged him not to put something down that wasn't true the next time he applied for a job.

Check out resumes before you hire people, and continue to check up on what they tell you after they come to work. Never take for granted that people are dealing with you truthfully. Often the people closest to you are frauds, hiding who they really are, not trusting that you could accept them as they are.

A winner finds a way to be honest and adds others who are honest. There is not security without the bond of honesty. If you don't give it to the people who work with you, they certainly are not going to give it to you.

2. Loyalty

In a day when many people are out for themselves with little thought for the livelihood of the organization or the person who has hired them, loyalty is an exceptional quality. Anyone coming to you with a resume consisting of fifteen jobs in ten years probably will show up at work looking for a better deal somewhere else. Loyal people stick around through thick and thin.

When I interview someone for a position, I like to ask how long the person can commit to the organization, no matter what happens. I ask him to commit at least one year before he entertains the idea that he may have made a mistake. I ask her to be sure of the decision before she decides to come on board, so she can focus on the job at hand, not on whether it was the right thing to do. I also pledge my loyalty to him. I stick to that pledge. I do a lot of work with a person before I decide that there is no way for the relationship to work out. Even though I know you have to move on mishires, those who know me know I err on the side of loyalty instead of quickly letting someone go. That may be why we have such an incredible team of loyal people who have been around a long time.

3. Positive Attitude

Earlier I wrote of the importance of attitude and the fact that in the midst of struggle, the only thing you are really up against is your own attitude. Optimism is essential for success. It is the ingredient that often allows the near impossible to be achieved. If I hire someone and find that the person was covering up a very negative attitude during the interview, I have to confront the person about it immediately and hope that I can motivate change. More often than not I can't. The person is too comfortable with the negative view of everything.

One of the people who used to work for me, during a time that my company struggled greatly, always said why something could not be done and interpreted every minor event as a catastrophe. If this person said a place was burning to the ground, we knew someone was probably playing with matches. The words coming out of this person's mouth were always negative and carried a doomsday tone. Not a lot gets done with negaholics around you.

One caution for a leader is to be sure to differentiate between a bad attitude and the facts. We don't like to hear bad news; in fact, we may become addicted to good news. When someone tells the truth and it isn't positive, we need to act on it and show appreciation to the person for taking the risk to be the bearer of bad tidings. Even if someone is delivering a negative message, it can be done in such a way that motivates rather than deflates. When someone tells me something is broken, I love to hear it as long as the person has a couple of ideas on how to fix it and how this might end up becoming the best thing that could have happened to us. Those kinds of ideas cannot be generated by a person with a negative attitude.

4. Effectiveness

Too often we place great value on the person who is efficient and too little on the person who is effective. Efficient people save money; effective people know how to make it with limited resources. Organizations need efficiency, but they win when the focus is on effectiveness.

When reviewing a resume, you will often see a list of positions held with nicely inflated titles. I don't want to know what position the person held and what the person was called; I want to know what that individual accomplished. If people can't tell me something significant that they did, other than hold down the job, they probably aren't going to do much better if they come to work with me. Effective people win; efficient people figure out all sorts of ways to reduce the allocation of resources that may be needed to succeed.

5. Problem-Solving Skills

I attended a motivational seminar one time with a fellow employee who was hard to motivate. He worked for me, but I was always feeling dragged down by him and his attitude. I felt like he expected me to convince him that we could win. That way he wouldn't have to find a way to win. At the seminar we were asked to write out our weaknesses, and I saw him write down problem solving. All the pieces of my confusing dilemma fit in place instantly. He didn't know how to solve problems, and he manipulated me into providing him with different approaches to the problems he faced. He did not stay with the company much longer after that.

I had the good fortune early in my life to work with some very great nurses. Their whole orientation to patient care was to find a way to solve the problem. I really didn't know how to solve problems until then. I certainly hadn't picked up the skill in any of the business courses I had taken over the years. Those women gave me a vital tool for winning. If you find people who can solve problems, latch onto them and don't let them go.

6. Self-Discipline

Self-discipline is the ability to delay gratification. Winners are able to put off doing what would feel good so they can do what is needed. This talent isn't to be confused with rigidity. That is a stifling and confining trait. Self-disciplined people know how to set a goal, define the steps to accomplish the goal, and take each step, even though each one might be more painful than the one before. When following up on references, be sure to ask if this person is self-disciplined. If this person has this quality, you will spend less time motivating and more time congratulating over an astonishing job done well.

7. Sense of Humor

A winner is always healthy enough to laugh at himself or herself and can spread that good humor to everyone else. Nothing puts people at ease the way a good sense of humor and laughter do. My father was a master at this. He always had a joke for everyone he met. He did a lot and made a lot of money without a degree but with an engaging personality that invited people to laugh. He passed that humor on to me, and in the speaking I have done, it has become my greatest asset. In business, finding some element of humor has helped me, even in the worst of times.

8. Perseverance

I have perseverance, and I got it from my dad along with his sense of humor. I have been fortunate to hire others with this drive to find some way, any way, to get the job done. If we can't go over it, around it, or through it, we'll blow it up or airlift it out of there. We have an attitude that there has to be some way to succeed if we just don't give up. I like to know what people have done to fail big and what they did to overcome that failure. I want to know the biggest obstacles they have come up against and what they did to beat the odds. People who give something a little attention and then wimp out quit before they have a chance to win.

9. Team Player

Winners know that in the counsel of many, there is much greater potential to problem solve. They love to work as a team, sometimes leading and sometimes executing others' orders. Team players motivate others to do their best while they find ways to contribute to the big win. You have either a one-man operation or a team, and most operations need a team to succeed. Loners and prima donnas give up and give in rather than work together with someone else to achieve great success. Be sure that the people around you like being around people and know how to work as a team.

10. Unwillingness to Make Excuses

Excuses have never paid a bill or earned a bonus check. The only thing that is important is the attainment of results. If someone has entrusted you with resources to multiply or operations to manage, any time spent developing an excuse is a waste of time. "Get the job done or get out of the way" is the rule of the winner. A winner would never stoop so low as to come up with a lame excuse when there just might be another way to approach the problem.

Surround Yourself with Winners

Winning comes from surrounding yourself with winners who see and feel your winning attitude. Winning isn't easy, and it will require expecting the exceptional while accepting people as human and frail and subject to mistakes. The following prayer reflects the heart of a compassionate winner who is surrounded by other winners:

Dear Lord, please help me

to accept human beings as they are—not yearn for perfect creatures;

to recognize ability—and encourage it;

to understand shortcomings—and make allowances for them;

to work patiently for improvement—and not expect too much too quickly;

to appreciate what people do right—not just criticize what they do wrong;

to be slow to anger and hard to discourage;

to have the hide of an elephant and the patience of Job;

to help them win rather than wait for them to lose;

to extend their reach upward as we reach out to each other as a team.

In short, Lord, please help me be a better leader surrounded by winners.

(source unknown)

It is also important to remember that everyone has some good qualities and the potential to become a winner. You may have a part in helping others bring out the winning qualities that lie within them in seed form. Look for the good in those around you, even those you might prefer not to be around. By affirming the positive in others and setting a good example, you can help others in the process of becoming winners.

Summary:
Qualities of a Winner

1. Winners are honest.
2. Winners are loyal.
3. Winners have a positive attitude.
4. Winners are effective.
5. Winners possess good problem-solving skills.
6. Winners exercise self-discipline.
7. Winners have a healthy sense of humor.
8. Winners persevere.
9. Winners are team players.
10. Winners are unwilling to make excuses.

CHAPTER SEVEN

Don't Let Your Wounds Interfere with Your Mission

Earlier I presented the concept that people who win may be propelled into the winner's circle by their wounds, wounds that they may have brought on themselves and wounds that may have been caused by others. It doesn't really matter how you got wounded; if you are wounded, it hurts.

Out of that hurt come various attempts at pain reduction. For winners, it seems that work provides the most tempting source of pain relief. Winners get caught up in their work to avoid the pain. But it seems to take more and more work and winning to keep the pain down. Trying harder usually means failing harder and quicker.

It doesn't have to be that way. Wounds can be healed, and the healed can win. Let's look at some symptoms indicating that your wounds might be propelling you out of the winner's circle and examine some ways to resolve them before wounds of a winner turn to wounds of a loser and interfere with your mission.

Are you performing at top efficiency? Are you feeling productive and positive? If not, your wounds of the past may be starting to catch up with you. When we internalize our hurts, disappointments, and offenses and they remain unresolved, they change into a low-grade depression. And they take their toll, both at work and at home. See if any of these danger signals relate to you:

- Procrastination
- Focus on approval
- Doubt, fear, or worry
- Lack of energy
- Loss of mission
- Nervous, frantic approach to tasks
- Irritability
- Difficulty concentrating and staying focused
- Severe mood swings
- Memory loss
- Difficulty sleeping
- Loss of appetite or severely increased appetite
- Sense of hopelessness
- Lack of interest in others
- Feeling like a second-class citizen
- Empty feelings, like a shell going through the motions with nothing on the inside
- Lack of purpose or mission
- Destructive, draining, and demanding relationships
- Self-obsession that alienates you from others
- Living in the past
- Financial stress due to irresponsibility
- Sex addictions
- Guilt

Don't Let Your Wounds Interfere

- False expectations that lead to disappointments
- Anger and resentment
- Fatigue from trying too hard
- Loneliness caused by self-isolation
- Excessive busyness

If these symptoms are cropping up in your life more and more frequently, you will want to discuss the situation with your spouse. Ask for your spouse's support during this difficult time as you seek help in resolving some of your wounds.

The story of your current wound may be very evident to you. You may have a clear understanding of when it happened, how it happened, and why it happened. Knowing all that may be a start, but it doesn't help with resolution. It places you in a kind of emotional limbo, stuck with the awareness but lacking the motivation to help yourself. You need your spouse to challenge you to get involved with the healing process before you no longer can decide to help yourself because the consequences of the buried pain are too great.

PERSEVERING WITH WOUNDS

Not everyone who is severely wounded is doomed to failure in the end. In case you are feeling like a lonely loser at the moment—wounded, discouraged, and ready to give up—let me tell you about a man who somehow managed to deal with his wounds in spite of everything. Take a look at this resume and see if you can figure out who it belongs to before you get to the end.

1832—Lost job
1832—Defeated in race for state legislature
1833—Failed in business
1834—Elected to state legislature
1835—Girlfriend died

1835—Nervous breakdown
1838—Defeated—speaker of state legislature
1843—Defeated—nomination for U.S. Congress
1846—Elected to Congress
1848—Lost renomination to U.S. Congress
1849—Rejected for position of land officer
1854—Defeated for U.S. Senate
1856—Defeated in nomination for U.S. vice presidency
1858—Defeated again for U.S. Senate
1860—Elected U.S. president

The man's name? As you probably figured out, it's Abraham Lincoln.

Even though he had a life of heartache and disappointment, he apparently found some way of dealing with his nearly endless list of day-to-day wounds. He learned how to courageously bounce back, time and again, until an assassin's bullet finally ended his struggles.

Whether you're hurt at home, at work, or in both places at once, get back up, dust yourself off, handle the problem until it's resolved, and try again. Think about Honest Abe's own philosophy about wounding criticism and personal hurts:

> If I were to try to read, much less answer, all the attacks made on me, this shop might as well be closed for any other business. I do the very best I know how—the very best I can; and I mean to keep doing so until the end. If the end brings me out all right, what is said against me won't amount to anything. If the end brings me out wrong, ten angels swearing I was right would make no difference.

Abe might have been wounded, but he certainly possessed a persevering attitude. He is a great example that wounded people don't have to fail to get over their wounds.

Don't Let Your Wounds Interfere

What we would want to overlook, we had best pay attention to, deal with, and resolve so that we, too, can lead lives that in the end, like Lincoln's, made a difference.

THE STRUGGLES OF LIFE

At one time or another, everyone struggles with

- fatigue from working too hard because someone else didn't work hard enough. Too many hours are spent at the desk and too few at rest.
- frustration with circumstances and people's behavior, either domestic or professional. Expectations are greater than people either can deliver or want to deliver.
- fault-finders with negative attitudes, insults, rudeness, and other interpersonal confrontations. These people have such a low view of themselves that they have to bring other people down to their level.
- frightening news that threatens the future, hearing that doomsday is just around the corner, just over the hill.
- failure, and the humiliation and conflicts it brings. Some big mistakes are hard to overlook or to see as learning experiences.

All of us have these struggles that go with the territory of being a human being. When the relationship at home is healthy, it would seem simple enough for couples to sit down and talk about each day's activities—the good, the bad, and the ugly. But it doesn't always work that way. For one thing, couples rarely have the time to sit and pour out their hearts to each other. For another, a fairly common scenario often arises

WINNING AT WORK

—common enough to be written about by numerous marriage counselors and relationship therapists:

- A man often goes into an emotional "cave" to recover from wounds. He withdraws. He gets quiet. He doesn't feel like talking it out until he has finished working it out.
- A woman often takes the man's self-imposed isolation personally. She feels shut out of his world—abandoned, isolated, rejected.

When this dynamic occurs, the trouble spills over into the home. It spreads. It intensifies. It reinvents itself. All of us are wise to make the extra effort to talk our troubles over at home and to help the family understand what's going on, no matter how bad it may be. In return, we hope there will be encouragement, constructive dialogue, and perhaps even prayer. The source of irritation at work can become the source of growing closer together at home if we take the time to share.

HURTS FROM HOME

When the wounded person gets hurt at home, certain steps need to be taken so the consequences of the conflict don't end up jeopardizing a job or creating additional problems at work. Wounded people want to retreat into their work, but that temptation must be resisted so resolution can come to the hurt. The following steps enable a conflict to end, a hurt to be resolved rather than fester into an infectious wound that destroys both work and home.

1. Hurts Need to Be Confronted

The easiest thing to do in the short run is to ignore something that hurts you. The temptation is to let it slide by, going unnoticed. When you do that, it is called emotional procrastination. You are refusing to have a conflict because conflict hurts. When you don't confront the issue, you deepen your own wound. You also destroy the potential depth of the relationship.

When my wife and I were first married, we thought the goal was to keep the peace. There were many things we did that hurt each other. We didn't confront those hurts, so rather than grow together, we grew separately alongside each other.

When we finally stopped avoiding conflict, we saw a whole new dimension to our relationship. Yes, there were tough times full of pain. During those times, we were distant from each other. Then when each of us started to see the perspective of the other person, we came back together. There was an ongoing cycle of moving apart and moving closer together. Our relationship became like a beautiful dance with rhythm and depth. When we moved closer, it was a richer closeness. It eliminated the stagnation from the marriage.

Most every marriage that dies, dies from disengagement. One or the other disengages, and then the consequences of the disengagement appear in the form of affairs, workaholism, and other problems. The key is to stay engaged and be willing to enter the relational dance that healthy marriages must maintain, even when it's painful.

2. Hurts Need to Be Discussed

Once a hurt is confronted, the tendency is to blame the other person or shame the other person. All that really needs to happen is to discuss the hurt. If you have been hurt, it is probably because the hurt tapped into your deeper, larger wound. The discussion needs to center on how you felt and what you experienced rather than what you assume might be the motive or intent of the hurtful action or statement.

Be sure you are in control of your discussion so that a small hurt to you doesn't end up killing the relationship. Withstand the temptation to strike back and retaliate. Diffuse your anger by discussing the issue with another person. Striking back will cause your small hurt to escalate the situation into a major war. Discussion allows you to share openly and honestly how you feel. Turning discussion into target practice is never appropriate.

3. Hurts Need to Be Resolved

Resolution means that you have experienced the hurt, shared your feelings, and moved to the next step in life. Too often people continue to focus on a simple hurt, ruining their lives. They take a small hurt and infect themselves with bitterness and resentment.

Resolution comes when you choose to forgive and forget. You must find a way to release the person from the bondage of having the event thrown back at him or her over and over again. Even though you were the one who was hurt, you must do the tough thing and the noble thing and let the event go, released from your mind and the relationship. Resolution involves the refusal to hold on to the hurt.

Of course, this is important at home, but it is equally important at work. Thousands of business deals are never completed because someone was unwilling to resolve a conflict. If you want to succeed, be sure you are a resolver. Otherwise you will spend your life trying to get even. And that is exactly what you will most likely do: get even. People who get even never seem to find a way to get ahead.

So at home and at work, get over it, and get on with it. Don't let your wounds interfere with your mission or rob you of the most meaningful aspects of life.

GETTING ON WITH IT

As mature individuals, we eventually stop focusing on what was and what might have been and get on with what is and what is to be. We change our way of living away from the "if onlys" to the reality that faces us each day. If you are having a problem with getting on with it, perhaps the following steps will further assist you in the resolution of your wounds so that current hurts won't always be dragging you back in them. If you want to live in the present and attain the future God has reserved uniquely for you, take these steps.

1. Explore Your "Hurt Trail"

As Dr. David Allen suggests in his book *In Search of the Heart,* a hurt trail is a list of the most painful incidents you can recall in your past. By writing down these wounding circumstances, you are able to bring them into your consciousness.

Sometimes our hurts are based on our perceptions of life. For example, I assumed I was underprivileged because our family was less affluent than others. Even if you think you may have misperceived or overreacted to something, list it. An honest evaluation of your feelings may reveal to you that things weren't as bad as they seemed, and that awareness may in itself be a step toward healing.

You probably know that very deeply wounded people, who have suffered great abuse, sometimes are unable to remember portions of childhood. Working on your hurt trail probably won't be a one-day job—but the process will probably reveal new memories. You may want to seek the assistance of a friend or a qualified counselor. If a caring and trusted family member is available to you, he or she could be extremely helpful in putting the pieces together.

2. Allow Yourself to Feel the Pain of Those Hurtful Times

Many of us have stuffed away the pain of the past— we've denied it, repressed it, or simply pretended we weren't hurt. Feeling the pain of our wounds is a cleansing experience, even though the emotions themselves may be intense and a little frightening. If you feel you can't face the pain alone, talk it over with a pastor, rabbi, counselor, or therapist. And remember, pain you feel is far less dangerous than pain you hide.

3. Forgive the Ones who Wounded You

By carrying bitterness in our hearts toward those who have wounded us, we hurt ourselves most of all. Medical research proves conclusively that repressed anger causes a number of illnesses and makes some physical conditions worse. By forgiving those who have hurt us, we release the emotions that bind us to the painful past. When physical and emotional health are the goal, forgiveness is not an option—it is a requirement. But remember, it's a process, not an event.

Self-forgiveness is a significant part of this process. All too often we are unwilling to release ourselves from the guilt and shame we feel over the past. We keep reliving our mistakes, bathing ourselves in regret, and refusing to let go. Perhaps we're trying to pay penance. There are times we need to stop and ask ourselves, Would I be this unforgiving of anyone else in the world?

Not only do we need to forgive others; we also need to forgive God. Now, that may sound strange since God has never done anything mean to us. There are those who are angry and bitter toward God because they feel they weren't protected by God. They are disturbed that the gift of free choice given to each individual was used to hurt them. They blame God for not making the world perfect and perfectly to their liking. If those are some of your thoughts and feelings toward God, forgive God and restore your relationship with the Creator of the universe.

4. Recognize Your Behavior Patterns to Compensate for the Pain from Past Wounds

You may discover that your pain has caused you to compensate by overstressing one of the three elements of success—mission, money, or meaning. Consider these examples of overcompensation:

- Men and women who came out of financially strapped homes may be fixated on wealth and possessions. Their focus is too much on money with little regard to the mission or the meaning of that mission.
- Men and women who came out of families that questioned their capability, value, or intelligence may be fixated on accomplishments. Their focus is too much on the mission and getting it done with little regard for the cost or the meaning behind it.
- Men and women who came out of abusive, unloving families may be fixated on emotional rewards. Their focus is too much on the meaning with little regard to the financial realities that exist or the mission that must be accomplished for the organization to succeed.

Can you see yourself in these patterns? Of course, there will be notable exceptions. Some people try to recapture the family environment rather than reverse it. Others may have philosophical reasons for overfocusing on one of the elements. But one thing is sure—overcommitment to work, to the exclusion of family, friends, and a balanced personal life, is workaholism. Workaholism further wounds the wounded. Whether the purpose of overworking is financial, achievement related, or simply fear driven, it is always a clear indication of unresolved woundedness.

Act now so that the woundedness stops with you instead of being passed on to children. Decide that you will become the transitional generation and that there will be no further pain inflicted from a pain that began generations ago. If you want to win, you need to lose the wounds. You lose them with determination to do the hard work of resolving them. Perhaps you need to add one element to your life's mission: healing the wounds of your past.

Summary:
Three Keys to Ending Conflict

1. Hurts need to be confronted.
2. Hurts need to be discussed.
3. Hurts need to be resolved.

Four Keys to Living in the Present
Without Interference from Wounds

1. Explore your "hurt trail."
2. Allow yourself to feel the pain of those hurtful times.
3. Forgive the ones who wounded you.
4. Recognize your behavior patterns to compensate for the pain from past wounds.

CHAPTER EIGHT

Your Mission Must Include Communicating Love

Jean was crying in the bedroom when Ben came upstairs at bedtime. He did a double take and said, "What on earth is wrong? Why are you crying?"

"Nothing's wrong!" she snapped, her words muffled by a soggy Kleenex.

Ben stared at his wife's red, swollen eyes. "Nothing's wrong? And you've gone through half a box of tissues?"

"Nothing you'd care about."

He sighed. "Try me."

"All right! It was my birthday today. You spent the day golfing with your buddies from work and the evening watching a basketball game. You didn't even get me a card."

Ben was stunned. "But I told you happy birthday the first thing this morning."

"Oh, thanks a million!" She glared at him in disbelief. "And that's it? You're a jerk, Ben!"

"Jean, listen to me. You told me three times this week and twice last week not to worry about your birthday. You said you didn't want anything, and you didn't care if we went out to dinner. That's exactly what you said."

Again, she gave him that disbelieving look. "And so you didn't even buy a card or flowers or anything? That's a cop-out. You knew I'd be hurt if you didn't do anything. And you intentionally—"

"Now, wait a minute! Am I supposed to be a mind reader or what? You're always saying I don't listen. So this time I listened. I did everything you said. And now I'm a jerk."

"You should have known I wanted you to do something even if I said not to. I just didn't want you to feel like you had to go out of your way. But I didn't mean for you to ignore the whole thing."

"I didn't ignore the whole thing, and I didn't go out of my way!" Jean started sobbing even more loudly at this point. Fortunately, Ben had the presence of mind to put his arms around her, hold her, and say, "I'm sorry I misunderstood."

Someone like Ben might very well have "Love my wife" as part of his mission statement. However, unless he diligently commits himself to making sure love is communicated, his mission will not be fulfilled.

The real problem between Ben and Jean was one of communication. She had been trying to remind him of her birthday by mentioning it several times. But since she didn't want to seem to be asking for anything, she repeatedly said, "But I don't want anything." Her agenda was that Ben would remember the birthday, and in his great devotion to her, he would overrule her request for no presents and no dinner, and he would amaze her with some wonderful surprise.

Ben, who is a bit obsessed with himself, was looking for an excuse not to trouble himself with his wife's birthday so he took his wife at her word. He should have known better. But he didn't think beyond her words, and she expected him to. His lack of actions confirmed to her that he really didn't care much for her, no matter what his words of apology would attempt to express. If the relationship is not right, the communication will not be right, either. Sometimes if we work on communication, we find that there is more hope for the relationship than we had assumed.

Communication is one of the biggest problems in relationships today. And it is equally significant in corporations. Carefully printed signs posting the warning "Assume Nothing" are visible in countless offices, and they are there for a reason: unless you ask all the right questions and listen carefully to the answers, you could be left in the dark about something very important.

Whether at home or at the office, you must work at and develop communications skills, or problems will invariably arise. And since your love relationship at home will be your foundation and the source of your encouragement and inspiration, you must manage it as well as, or better than, your work relationships.

What are some of the ways you can learn to communicate openly with your spouse? The first essential is that you want to communicate. If your spouse is your best friend, you'll be anxious to share your daily life with her or him. Schedule in a regular phone call to the one you love. You can always take a minute to write a note if it guarantees a companion for a lifetime.

It's not good enough, however, just to say, "I love you. See you at six." Sharing life's ups and downs is part of the equation. Never let problems at work build up without at least discussing them at home. That way the one you love feels a part of the success or failure that is ahead.

People fear communication because they

- fear conflict.
- don't know how to say what they mean.
- can't handle criticism.
- have experienced abuse.
- aren't sure of the issues.
- want to seem cooperative.
- have an unspoken agenda.
- are afraid to lose.

These are not good reasons to evade any kind of conversation, whether it be casual, deep, or constructive dialogue. However, it's wise to remember that a quiet, pensive man or a woman of few words may not fear communication at all. He or she may find too much talk tedious and unnecessary. Personality differences have a great deal to do with whether or not conversations ever get started or last more than thirty seconds. If the "opposites attract" syndrome has matched you up with a noncommunicator, you may be faced with one of those unchangeable facts of life. Rather than struggle to change your partner, you may need to confront the golden silence with a measure of serene acceptance.

If you're afraid of saying the wrong thing, bear in mind that there are some words that can never go wrong when they are spoken in sincerity and love:

- Words of specific compliment
- Words of concern and warning
- Words of personal praise
- Words of confidence
- Words of trust
- Three little words: I love you

Although we all struggle with communication, some of us have mastered the art of it a little better than others. From those who know how to do it fairly well I have gathered some pointers that may be useful.

FIVE PRINCIPLES FOR GOOD COMMUNICATION

1. Empathize

The best response to another person expressing feelings is either "I understand" or "I don't understand." Our tendency is to want to give an answer rather than be understanding. When my father died, I didn't need anyone to help me figure it out. I needed someone to express concern and love, but I didn't need perspectives on death. I didn't need anyone to tell me why it happened. I just needed someone to be there. Being there is just as powerful a positive communication as not being there is a negative communication.

2. Use "I" and "You" Statements Appropriately

When attempting to communicate about a problem, use "I" statements rather than "you" statements. State that this is how "I" feel rather than point a finger about what "you" did or should have done.

Use "you" statements when trying to accurately communicate to the other person who is expressing a concern to you. When you do this, you increase the chance for accurate communication by about 100 percent while at the same time demonstrating that you truly care about the other person's concern.

3. Recognize the Power of Words

This is a tough one for people in power. Some people will feel good or bad, perform well or poorly, based on the words you express to them. All people have a need to be noticed, and the words from those in charge have the powerful ability to validate people or negate their importance. Be sure there are no backhanded compliments, and ensure that if a person is within speaking distance, you speak to that person. Additionally, the easiest way to increase the value of any company is to increase the value of every employee. This is done with words of praise, encouragement, and gratitude.

4. Speak the Truth in Love

Anytime you have to correct a person, you are showing love if you correct him or her in the right way. The absence of love is indifference. A person who is going to the trouble to conduct a painful confrontation rather than take the easy way and ignore it is providing a loving opportunity for change. But do not take the opportunity and destroy the person with words spoken in haste. Take the time to calm the anger and irritation before talking to the person. Be sure that your motive is to help the company and to help the person grow and develop into a more productive employee.

5. Listen

Listening has to be the most important communication skill. If you are in charge of an operation, there is a good chance you are not listening to the truth. One reason is that people don't want to tell you the truth. Either they want to protect you from the truth, or they want to protect themselves by keeping you from knowing it.

The second reason you probably aren't listening to the truth is that as you get to the top of the organization, you tend to take less time to listen. Be sure you take the time; force yourself to find ways to stay in touch with reality through sessions where you are determined to hear the truth, even if it isn't what you want to hear.

Listening is important to communication for many reasons. Let's examine some of them.

Poor listening skills are responsible for a tremendous

waste in education, industry, and relationships. Consider the many young people who graduate from high school without comprehending the basics of a good education. It is not that they were not taught. Other students sitting in the same class-room come away with real understanding. What made the difference between being prepared and being unprepared is that one listened and learned while others did not listen and did not learn. Every time you do not listen you forfeit the opportunity to learn something.

Listening makes effective leadership possible. When people know they have been heard, they are far more likely to follow your lead. Listening shows that you value the input of those under your leadership. You may not always choose to do what they want, but if they know you have heard them and have taken their views into consideration, they will be far more likely to follow willingly.

Listening is vital to building relationships. Relationships require interaction between two human beings. When another person opens up to share something of himself with you, you must listen carefully to understand him. If someone dares to reveal a part of her inner self and you do not meet the offering with the courtesy to listen, further steps toward building rela-tionship will be halted.

Listening brings people into community. When you listen and respond to others, showing that you understand their concerns, you find areas you hold in common. This common ground is the basis for community. Your willingness to listen to others and identify common ground brings you into com-munity with them. Even avowed enemies can at times find areas of agreement if they listen to each other long enough.

All forms of psychotherapy emphasize that listening is probably the most simple and effective single technique for helping troubled people. You can help those you love, comfort those in sorrow, and encourage downcast souls by listening as they share their troubles. When you listen, you allow others to sort through their feelings and thoughts with a sense of being validated. You help them realize their troubles are worth hearing and mourning.

Taking the time to listen shows you love someone with your attention and presence. You communicate love by how you spend your time. Those who love golf spend their Saturdays on the golf course. Those who love food spend time eating a lot of it. If you love a person, you will spend time with that person or do things on behalf of that person. You communicate your love with your presence; it is the communication that those who love you will always prefer. When it comes to love, you just can't phone it in. Make sure you communicate love with your presence as well as in other ways.

WHEN SOMEONE YOU LOVE IS WINNING AT WORK BUT LOSING YOUR LOVE

Perhaps you are in a relationship with a person who is winning at work but is in danger of losing your love. It may be your father or mother. It may be your spouse or the person you are engaged to marry. The person you have in mind when we talk about winning at working and losing at love needs to know how you feel. You may be able to help the person become a winner in all aspects of life by communicating your love and helping him or her see the imbalance.

Here are some things you can do when someone you love is winning at work but losing your love:

- Communicate your concerns without attacking character. If you are dealing with a workaholic who has insecurity issues, attacking the person's life may only drive a wedge between you. Instead, communicate that you love and appreciate the dedication at work but desire the same kind of dedication at home.

- Be willing to seek guidance, especially if the person you are concerned about is your spouse or fiancé(e). Licensed marriage counselors are skilled at helping couples work through the surface issues and identify underlying issues the workaholic may be incapable of seeing without assistance.
- If the person being consumed by work is also frustrated by the way the demands of work interfere with your relationship, work together to come up with ideas of how to make a change. If you attack the person for the lack of involvement with you, you lose the opportunity to team up with him or her to come up with alternatives that bring balance to both lives.
- Don't look to any one person to fulfill your social and emotional needs. While the one you love is neglecting your relationship, develop same-sex relationships that offer you companionship, support, and comfort. Consider the possibility that you may be demanding more than the other person can reasonably supply for you. A variety of relationships with other family members and friends can help fill the void until your loved one gains a healthy balance in life.
- Don't use the absence of involvement as an excuse for not living a full life. Don't blame another for your lack of fulfillment. Take responsibility for your own life. Do what you can to change yourself in ways that help you live a balanced life. One of the best ways to bring about positive change in a relationship is to change yourself and stop harping about the shortcomings of the other person.
- Consider confrontation. A workaholic may be as

out of control as an alcoholic. If several members of the person's family and circle of friends recognize that workaholism is negatively affecting relationships, they can join together to intervene. The people prepare statements, showing how the workaholism is affecting their lives. Then they communicate how this makes them feel and what it means to them that the person works so much while neglecting the relationships. If the problem is severe enough to warrant counseling, select a counselor, and strongly urge the person to seek counseling. If there are consequences on the horizon, don't use them as idle threats, but let him or her know what is at risk.

The Bible says we should speak the truth in love. Most of us hesitate to confront difficult situations with people we love. However, sometimes the hard truth, spoken out of a genuine concern for the relationship, is the most appropriate demonstration of love.

Summary:
Five Principles for Good Communication

1. Empathize.
2. Use "I" and "you" statements appropriately.
3. Recognize the power of words.
4. Speak the truth in love.
5. Listen.

Part 3

The Money

CHAPTER NINE

What Money Is and Isn't

As anyone who has ever had money knows, it does not buy happiness. Nonetheless, most of us want more and fiercely protect what we've acquired. Given a choice of having money or not having it, I'd like to have it. The problem is not in having money; the problem comes if it has you. Money handled poorly can eat a person alive and destroy a lifetime of accomplishments.

Unless you are independently wealthy, achieving some sort of financial gain will necessarily be part of your life's mission. You have to support your family. You have to meet your obligations. You have to eat! And if you are like me, there are children who want to go to college, and that takes a lot of green stuff today and will take even more in the days ahead.

In our very materialistic culture the meaning of money goes well beyond the provision of daily bread. Possessions, prestige, and power have to do with net worth, and these allurements are almost hypnotic in their appeal. Not only is our appetite for more insatiable, but a sense of entitlement often accompanies success. If we're not careful, we may acquire a certain arrogance along with our big checks. Who hasn't encountered the nouveau riche individual who wears the fashionable tokens of wealth like so many badges of honor? If you are like me, the show of wealth never impresses you. The person who really impresses me is the one I know has a lot but shows very little of what is there.

What is most important about money is not how much you make but how much you keep. This is one of the early lessons I learned the hard way. I always judged a person's success by the amount of the paycheck. Then I discovered that salary is the poorest indicator of financial success. The guy who makes $100,000 a year, but owes $200,000 in short-term debt that must be paid off immediately, is failing miserably and is most likely very miserable. The real success is the $30,000-a-year postal worker or teacher who retires with a pension and $1 million in a portfolio because of spending just a little less than the amount made. The more you keep, the more you can make once you retire and no longer have a fat paycheck. Too often I have seen the big spender in youth be the pauper in older age.

The fact is, most of us aren't really tempted to try to become a redesigned Donald Trump; we are more likely drawn toward that ever-ellusive 25 percent more-than-what-we-have. The classic John D. Rockefeller quote is worth repeating. When asked how much money is enough money, he smiled and said, "Just one dollar more!"

TOO FOCUSED ON FINANCES

Most of us could use another dollar, but if the reason we implement a mission is only for the sake of money, the money will provide us with little satisfaction. Anytime money becomes an end unto itself, it seems to poison an individual or a family. When money is seen as a means to an end, such as a way to give something back, its richness increases while its sting diminishes. In search of just one dollar more, a person is likely to never be content with what he or she is making. The real goal should be finding contentment with what we have, even though we hope to be making more in the future.

In business, people are usually either very money centered or very people centered. If you are money centered, people will question your motives as manipulative and motivated only by accumulating more wealth for yourself. If you are money centered and materialistic, people will recognize that, and they will reject you, even if there is a big heart accompanying your money-centered mind. Here are characteristics that may be associated with the money-centered person:

- Insecurity. People know that in and of yourself, you do not feel like a whole person. You need the addition of material goods to make yourself feel good. Anytime your ability to make money is threatened, you revert to your negative backup style that is demanding and self-centered.
- Confused priorities. You would place profit over people. You have become so money centered that little affects you compassionately. You judge others primarily on the basis of how much they earn. You care more about the figures than the feelings of the people being influenced by financial decisions.
- Impaired judgment. Because of your impaired judgment, you will make your decisions on how the most money can come in with the least amount of trouble. In doing this your blind spots may keep you from seeing other elements that

could add to the overall success of a given project. Your focus on the bottom line may keep you from seeing all contributing factors.

• Strength. Your sense of personal strength and worth is directly linked to how much money you make. The more you make, the stronger you feel. When the money dries up, you are destined to feel weak and make poor decisions out of weakness. Anyone can act strong when full of money, but it takes the person of character to be able to be strong when the money is no longer there. Strength from money is always fleeting.

THE OTHER SIDE OF THE COIN

There is another approach to finances that doesn't help us win at work or at love. That is to approach life without focusing on finances at all. Some individuals, like our friend Don in chapter 1, refuse to give any attention to money making at all. These are the ones who act as though making and managing money are optional. Perhaps they are lazy. Maybe they feel incompetent about finances and would rather not think about them. Or they might be philosophically committed to the idea that money is a by-product of good intentions. These people may see money as evil, and they pride themselves on their lack of money, as if they have taken some vow of poverty. No matter—people who refuse to include money in their overall life mission are forever struggling to make ends meet.

If you have spent your life avoiding money issues, never learning money management skills, you need to face this as a problem to be solved. There is some reason you have avoided this essential part of life in the real world. The sooner you face the problem, the better off you will be in your attempts to win at work and at home. Left unexamined and uncorrected, this lack of attention to finances will be a source of lifelong problems.

One friend with whom I collaborated on a book about codependency issues realized in the writing of the book that she had completely ignored anything associated with money management. She had a pattern of working for substandard pay in ministry positions. She justified her lack of money with the thought that she was sacrificing her life for a noble cause. However, that did not explain her aversion to everything associated with personal finance. She never balanced her checkbook, refused to keep account of spending, and in every way imaginable tried to act as though money does not make the world go round.

As the writing project continued, she took time to consider why this important part of her life was void. Based on this careful reflection, she associated her aversion to money issues with a childhood of uncertainty caused by her father's compulsive gambling and financial mismanagement. She then was able to see that her reaction to money problems was inappropriate. She chose to deal with the emotional problems as such, and she committed herself to accepting responsibility for handling finances conscientiously. She also began to change her mind about money, learning to see that it can be a source of family security and provision rather than a source of pain and shame. My friend chose to make changes, overcoming her lack of knowledge with small, wise, and dedicated steps. As a result, her income increased four times over, she and her husband purchased a home they previously believed out of reach, and her life at work and at home is greatly improved all around.

EVALUATING YOUR RELATIONSHIP WITH MONEY

Barbara Walters asked Ted Turner, "What does it feel like to be so wealthy?"

He said, "It's like a paper bag. Everyone sees the bag. Everyone wants it. Once you get the bag, you discover that the bag is empty."

Isn't it amazing how many people are giving up the joy of life while striving for something that will amount to nothing more than an empty paper bag and a continuing search for fulfillment? You would think that Ted Turner, one of the richest men of our time, should know about having money.

His comments are reminiscent of those of another wealthy man from another time. King Solomon is estimated to have been the wealthiest man in the world when he penned these words:

> He who loves silver will not be satisfied with silver;
> Nor he who loves abundance, with increase.
> This also is vanity.
> When goods increase,
> They increase who eat them;
> So what profit have the owners
> Except to see them with their eyes? (Eccl. 5:10–11).

Amazing! These two wealthy men, separated by time and culture, tell us essentially the same thing: don't be deceived; having more money may not meet your expectations. That is why we need to evaluate how we feel about money. If we take the time to check our monetary attitudes, we have a greater chance of working toward something more meaningful than an empty paper bag. Reevaluate your attitudes related to money by responding to the following questions and statements.

WINNING AT WORK

1. Do you think, *If I only had an extra few thousand dollars, my problems would be solved?* If so, that's backward. Money may help you get the things you value, but it won't help you determine what those things are. Write a short paragraph on your feelings about what you value and hope to purchase with the money you have and the money you hope to make.

2. Rethink your attitudes toward money—what it's for, what it can do, and why you want it and need it. Consider how you use money. Do you use it to compensate for other areas where there is a lack that is not financial? For example, do you give your children money or gifts to compensate for your guilt over not spending enough time with them? Do you buy your spouse gifts as an expression of love or as a guilt offering?

   To help you rethink your attitudes about money, make a list of how you spent your discretionary money in the last month. After each item, write out what kind of need you were trying to fill with the expenditure: emotional, status, stress reduction, social acceptance, compensation for feelings of deprivation, and so on. Then ask yourself if there is a more appropriate way to meet each need. Determine if your money is serving you well or if you are in bondage to your finances because of inappropriate spending. What needs attention to keep you from spending inappropriately?

3. What is important to you? Make a random wish list of things you'd like to have. (Enter a separate item on each line.) Most people carry around such a list in their minds, consisting of their latest needs and desires. Think hard. Take your time. This discovery process is crucial, and it amounts to a sort of money mission statement. It helps you focus on what you really want.

If you're married, get your spouse involved. Have your spouse make a list. You may prevent future arguments over finances if you understand each other's wants and needs and then negotiate a shared set of priorities.

4. Now go back and assign a ranking to these wishes, making sure you know the difference between those that are essential, those that are important, and those that are on the frivolous side. You assign value to the items by prioritizing them in importance. Some that are the most important may not be the most expensive. Value and cost do not always correlate.

5. Evaluate the cost of each item in terms of time, energy, and money. Everything you have or achieve will cost you a combination of these three elements. If you want to save time, you usually have to spend more money for the convenience. A microwavable dinner doesn't cost more than a homemade dinner because it has more valuable ingredients. It costs more because it saves the consumer time and energy (both valuable commodities). You can choose to spend more time and energy to save money or vice versa. Now determine how much it will cost to reach each goal, deciding how much time, energy, and money you are willing to spend. Go back and put a price tag on each item listed.

6. Decide the time frame in which you plan to reach each goal. Some things that are very important may take longer to work toward, while some things that are less important may cost less and therefore can be reached sooner. Set a date by which you intend to meet each goal. Give your goals deadlines.

7. Time and money must interact responsibly if you are to keep your balance. You decide how to use your time and money to achieve the goals that you value. If you choose to give yourself unrealistic deadlines for reaching your financial goals, you set yourself up to fail in other areas of life that require your participation. You control the chosen time frame in which to reach your goals. Be careful to make time for the other elements of life that contribute to your mission and meaningful relationships. In the space below, figure out what you would have to do every week to meet your goals. What do you have to do every month? Break your goals into a weekly or monthly plan of action with specific tasks noted that will be steps toward fulfilling your goals. Allocate your money to specific goals and needs.

GOD AND MONEY

If God is in charge of your money, God is in charge of your life. If God is not in charge of your money, chances are, He does not reign in your life. God really does care about your money. It is notable that the Bible mentions prayer in about four hundred places, but it mentions money in about two thousand places. You may often leave God out of your money-making and giving decisions, but you should not. Integrating your faith and finances is essential to fulfillment in life.

It makes sense that God would care so much about money since one of the most perilous threats to faith in God and dependence on Him seems to be a fat paycheck. People who were close to God when they had to pray "give us this day our daily bread" may stray from Him when their needs are not as immediate. I believe that for some who have wandered away from God when the money was flowing in abundance, the best thing that can happen to their faith in God is to have financial difficulties. This circumstance may be what it takes to remind them of their dependence on God. However, you can maintain your dependence on God while being blessed financially if you have the right perspective.

Having more than enough is not the only snare. People who live in poverty or frequently lack money may perceive God as being uncompassionate. They may fault God for their financial circumstances and therefore avoid a relationship with Him.

It is not the amount of money you have or don't have that matters most to God or determines that your attitude toward money is right. What determines whether or not your attitude toward money is correct is the place it holds in your affections. Some people wrongly believe that money is the root of all evil. The Bible actually says, "The love of money is a root of all kinds of evil, for which some have strayed from the faith in their greediness, and pierced themselves through with many sorrows" (I Tim. 6:10).

I see two common denominators that indicate a wrong attitude toward money regardless of the amount. People who have a wrong perspective about money lack contentment, and are always greedy for more, and they envy others who appear to have more than they do.

1. God Cares How You View Money

Many men and women look at money as the number one priority in life. According to Scripture, God wants us to view it somewhere behind Him and our families. God doesn't want us obsessed with anything that brings on so many problems and of itself has no eternal value. Jesus challenged a rich young ruler to give away all he had to the poor and then follow Him. The man went away extremely sad because he was unwilling to give away his earthly riches. Jesus did not ask everyone to give away possessions. However, he wanted the young man to recognize the supreme place his riches held in his heart. Jesus knew that for some of us money must be dethroned before God can have His rightful place in our lives.

Are you able to give freely? Jesus taught that we should be able to give to those who ask and never turn our backs on those who want to borrow. If this thought is reprehensible to you, you need to reexamine how you view money. God wants us to view money as a gift from Him and trust that He will provide enough. He wants us to have enough faith to cheerfully give a portion of whatever He has provided.

The most vivid lesson I learned about giving and faith came when Sandy and I visited a small village in India. The cardboard shacks were scattered along a sewage-filled ditch. Most of the adults in the poverty-stricken community were severely disabled. They grew up being used to evoke pity from tourists while their parents begged. The more severely disabled the child, the more money the parents could attract. Some of them had to crawl on all fours because of disabilities inflicted on them by their parents in the struggle to survive.

Their lives as adults were not significantly better than those of their parents. Poverty kept their children as beggars, too. And yet when we went to their church meeting, the people joyfully gave a portion of their meager earnings to the Lord. They had great delight in showing their recognition of God's provision and faith in His future provision by giving back a portion of what little they had. No matter how little we think we have, our view of money should be such that we can freely give a portion to God and others in greater need.

2. God Cares How You Accrue Money

Recently, the *Los Angeles Times* business section reported the demise of a successful Orange County company that was the darling of Wall Street. It was losing money every day. Its stock plummeted as it looked for someone to buy what there was left of the business. At the top of the corporation was a man addicted to greed. Here's what the article said:

What Money Is and Isn't

"Interviewing an ex-employee, the employee said that the people resented the head of the company because he paid below standard wages, yet he drove a Rolls Royce and had a home in both Palm Springs and Newport Beach." A godly understanding of money allows no room for greed and oppression of others.

Keep the following points in mind about accruing money:

- Don't cheat your workers out of their wages. When Moses gave the law of God to the people of Israel, he made it clear that oppression of persons working for you is wrong. He said, "You shall not oppress a hired servant who is poor and needy, whether one of your brethren or one of the aliens who is in your land within your gates. Each day you shall give him his wages, and not let the sun go down on it, for he is poor and has set his heart on it; lest he cry out against you to the LORD, and it be sin to you" (Deut. 24:14–15).

- Don't cheat your family through workaholism. You can choose the rate at which you accrue your money. If you are neglecting your family commitments in your quest for financial success, you are out of line. Take more time with your family, even if it takes more time to reach your career and financial goals.

- Don't cheat the government with false tax returns. You may be tempted to cheat the government by justifying this action on the basis that everyone else does it or that you don't approve of how the government uses your money. Honesty is essential in all of life, but it is most easily seen or seen lacking in financial dealings. If you are not being honest about your taxes, you are in error. Your faith in God should help you trust that He can provide for you on your income after taxes. If you don't agree with how your tax dollars are being spent, take appropriate political action; don't use this as an excuse for cheating.

• Don't cheat your employer. Most people don't embezzle money from their companies. However, many cheat their employers in other ways. You can cheat your employer by taking office supplies, wasting time the employer is paying you to use in service to the company, or taking liberties with use of company telephones, products, or other office services. Some people begin taking these kinds of liberties when they feel they are not being compensated enough. If you want more for what you do, negotiate it; don't take it.

3. God Cares How You Go Through Money

God wants you to spend your money by investing it wisely. Money is a gift, and God expects you to take the gift and multiply it. If you hold on to something God wants you to use, you have wasted the money and the opportunities for increase it could have afforded you.

Jesus told a story of a man who went away on a trip, but before leaving, he gave three of his servants a sum of money. The first two invested their money and received a return on their investments. The third didn't invest the money for fear of losing it and displeasing the master, whom he saw as a demanding man. He buried his money in the ground, thinking he was doing something great by making sure he didn't lose it. However, when the master returned, the man who failed to invest his money was severely reprimanded, and the little he had was taken away.

God wants you to trust Him enough to gain confidence that will help you take the prudent risks necessary to make a

What Money Is and Isn't

profit. He does not want you to live in the kind of financial fear that causes you to hide your money away without putting it to productive use.

God also wants you to spend wisely and reserve a portion of your income for giving wisely. When you give, remember to give generously, anonymously, and voluntarily.

When you go through your money, God wants you to invest it, spend it, and give it wisely. Whether in tipping, taxes, T-bills, or tithing, go through your money wisely.

I hope you are balanced in your view of what money is and what it isn't, what it can do and what it cannot do. When you are mature in your attitudes toward money, you realize that money can't make you happy, but having right attitudes toward money can help you enjoy your happiness.

Summary:
God and Money

1. God cares how you view money.
2. God cares how you accrue money.
3. God cares how you go through money.

CHAPTER TEN

Money as a Family Affair

If you spend all of your time investing your money and little time investing your love, there is a good chance that you will end up with a lot of time to count your money alone. Money is one of the major sources of friction in a family. How family members deal with money often robs a family of the love that was there before the money came along. There can also be significant difficulties in a family when the level of income dips unexpectedly and family members have to learn to manage during times of financial insecurity.

There are ways you can ensure that money issues don't rob you of your family. One basic way is to be sure you are not wasting unnecessary emotions on arguing over money and how it is spent. The following tips will help you avoid major friction over money issues.

EIGHT TIPS FOR AVOIDING FAMILY FIGHTS OVER MONEY

1. Know Your Spouse's Financial Personality as Well as Your Own

Spenders tend to marry savers, but they become very uncomfortable with their differences when the monthly statements start rolling in. Talk through each of your priorities, and make sure you aren't competing for control. One person may be more adept at paying the bills. Allow each person to use skills to corporately manage family finances. However, you don't have to make one person solely responsible for financial goals and management. Allow for each person's view of money, and set the guidelines mercifully, based on the unique traits of each individual.

2. Keep Checking, Savings, Investments, and Credit Cards in Joint Accounts

This approach keeps big spenders from springing big surprises on their spouses. One of the worst decisions is to marry someone who wants to keep a separate financial life. Marriage needs to be a complete union, especially in merging money. I believe that every prenuptial agreement is an annulment document that prevents a complete marriage from ever occurring. If you are thinking of marrying someone who doesn't want your hands on his or her money, it might be best to withdraw your hand from the prospect of marriage.

My wife and I have several friends who have signed prenuptial agreements, keeping finances separate. At first it wasn't an issue, but as the years have gone by, those agreements, still in force, are a major source of irritation. One woman feels as if the marriage has never occurred and she is there only as a cook and a sexual partner. A wall between them is destructive to the partnership. I believe it will be that way until they become completely married, financially as well as physically.

3. Keep All Debt Below 35 Percent of Your Gross Income

I will never forget the feeling I had after I had purchased new carpeting, a new television set, and new furniture. It was my first foray into the use of credit. I bought the carpet on one of those deals where you pay 18 percent interest over ten years and end up paying for the carpet four times over. But the low monthly payment was awfully, and I mean awfully, inviting. I couldn't keep the old television set in a room with new carpet, so I bought a new Sony and it was beautiful. It was so beautiful, it made my furniture look really bad. So I charged some new furniture. Before I was finished, the low monthly bill was more than I could ever manage. So I ended up with a debt consolidation loan that took me ten years to pay off at $87 a month. I can still remember the last payment I made on that bill.

Whatever you do, don't ruin your life with credit. If you carry a balance of $3,300 and pay the minimum payment every month, it will take you ten years to pay off your debt. If you are a habitual credit card abuser, get some help, and find out what it is inside you that is driving you to destroy your security and your relationship with your spouse. It can become just as addicting as alcohol, so don't wait before you have charged your future away.

4. Agree On and Plan for Joint Financial Goals

Some folks have to set goals before they can agree on them. If one of you wants to have a life of luxury now and the other one wants to have a relaxing retirement, you are going to have recurring money conflicts. Sit down and discuss your values, hopes, and dreams. Then compromise and plan until both agree on a balance between conflicting goals.

5. Have Periodic, Scheduled Summit Meetings About Family Finances

Just as you cannot effectively reach goals and control costs in business without regular meetings where managers and those working together look at the financial situation, you cannot effectively reach family goals and control costs without working together with accurate, up-to-date information about family finances. I suggest a family business meeting once a month or every two weeks. In this meeting look at how you are doing compared to your goals (including your budget). You will need accurate information about family income, expenditures for the month, and the status of debts. Use this information to help each family member see which areas need improvement and areas where you are doing a good job managing finances. Be sure to recognize and applaud your successes as well as correct your errors. At the end of the meeting, compile an action list of items that need attention and who will make sure these are completed. At the next meeting, review the previous month's list to confirm all commitments were fulfilled.

Open part of your meeting to your children. Often parents keep family finances a mystery. Therefore, children don't understand why lights need to be turned off or the thermostat for the air conditioner needs to be set at a higher temperature. Through these summit meetings, children can learn that money wasted will not be available to them for discretionary spending. This can motivate them to keep expenses down. The sooner they learn the responsible decisions you are making, the more likely they will be mature with money. The summit provides a regular opportunity for you to show them the hows and whys of your financial decision-making process.

6. Agree on a Budget and Work Together on Keeping It

I think this is the tough one because people go to one of two extremes, neither of which is satisfactory. One extreme is to spend by the seat of your pants whenever you feel like spending. You just spend and hope at the end of the day there will be some way that it will all work out. The other extreme is to decide to count every penny and implement a system so cumbersome that no one can follow it and everyone gives up quickly.

A better approach is to see how much money is allocated to each ongoing expense, how much must be held back for future expenses, and how much is left. Then spend what is left as desired. In this way the spending is contained but not so rigidly that the system is abandoned.

If you really struggle with any system, you may want to implement an old-fashioned envelope system that works well. Allocate money to the fixed expenses and then place the rest in envelopes. If you have one hundred dollars left, cash a check for one hundred dollars and place an amount in the eating-out envelope and an amount in the entertainment envelope and all the other categories you can think of. If you don't have enough to spend in a category, you will have to wait another month until the cash balance builds up. This system has worked for many families when nothing else would. It may be old-fashioned, but it's effective.

7. Don't Commit Family Money to an Investment or a Debt Without Consulting Your Spouse

This advice is self-explanatory. Use your marriage partner as an investment partner. If you tend to make impulsive decisions, knowing you need to talk it over with your spouse forces you to take your time. Often investment decisions are based on emotions, and this step allows your emotions to settle down. It also provides you with a way out, telling the person that you must consult your business partner before moving forward on an investment. If the investment fails, at least both of you were in it together.

8. Invest in Things That Make Both of You Feel Comfortable

Be sure the risk of an investment isn't so high that it robs you of your peace of mind. Less risk with less reward but more relaxation and peace is a better equation than high risk that could take all your money away. Partnering in an investment, weighing the pros and cons of it, is a way to grow your love while you grow your money.

TEACHING KIDS ABOUT MONEY

If you have kids, teaching them how to be responsible with money is very important. At three years old my daughter Madeline knows that the reason I go to work is to get money so we can pay for the house. She began saving a portion of the money we gave her, and she enjoys giving some away to the church. When she is older, we will communicate regularly with her about our financial status.

Your children are watching you and depending on you to prepare them to succeed in life. If you do not teach them the basics of money management, there is no assurance they will pick them up along the way. It is your job to guide them as they grow up in a world where money management is essential.

Here are some basic concepts that even young children can begin learning in your home:

- There is no free lunch. Work brings financial rewards. If you don't work, you should not expect pay. Children can begin doing simple household chores as early as three years of age. Their efforts can be rewarded financially. If they fail to complete their chores, they should not receive their allowance.

- Whenever there is income, some of that money is to spend, some to save, and some to give away. Neale S. Godfrey, the author of *Money Doesn't Grow on Trees,* suggests using three jars into which all money is divided. One jar is for spending money (for the child to use on things like treats from the ice-cream truck, video games, or toys). Another jar is for short-term savings, and a third is for long-term savings (primarily for college). Godfrey's two children were featured with her on Oprah Winfrey's show. Both had accrued over five thousand dollars (a portion of money they earned) to be used toward college expenses. All this at the ripe old ages of eight and eleven! They began earning and saving money at age three. I would add a jar to put away money to give to the church or a specific cause.

- Each person can make a significant contribution by giving to others who are less fortunate. Several families I know allow each of their children to sponsor a child through one of many fine organizations like Compassion International, World Vision, or the Christian Children's Fund. They choose children the same age and sex as themselves. Each month they send a portion of the twenty-some dollars it takes to clothe and feed a child in a developing country. The children exchange pictures and correspondence. In this way they are connected to other children in other circumstances in a way that inspires compassion. These children learn to appreciate the blessings they have while discovering the joy of helping others.

- Education allows you to work smarter, not harder. When one of my friends was trying to encourage her oldest child to read, she struck upon the idea of offering to pay the girl to read stories to her younger brother and sister. She much preferred this idea to her other optional chore. The girl approached her reading with fresh enthusiasm, and she learned that an education allowed her to make money in a way that was interesting and pleasurable.

Consider the following seven ways to instill good financial character in kids.

1. Set a Good Example

Your kids need to see you in action with your money. They need to see you spend money wisely, save money wisely, and occasionally buy something fun and rewarding for all the hard work you do. Most important, they need to see you give your money wisely. Children who get caught up in responsible giving see the accumulation of money not only as a means of future security but as an opportunity to help others. Be sure they see your character in each transaction you make with your money.

2. Provide a Regular Allowance

Kids need to be considered contributing members of the family. They are entitled to some of the rewards for doing their part to keep the household running and in order. They need a small regular portion of money so that they can learn how to manage it and turn a little money into a lot more money. A good rule of thumb suggested by Neale S. Godfrey in *Money Doesn't Grow on Trees* is one dollar of pay per year of age per week. A three-year-old child is assigned chores at her ability level and receives three dollars per week if the chores are done. A ten-year-old has more responsibility and more difficult chores, so he receives ten dollars per week.

When your children receive an allowance, allow them to use it for miscellaneous expenses. If they overspend and don't have money to spend when the other kids are racing out the door to the ice-cream vendor, let them learn from experience the negative effects of running out of money. Don't always be there to bail them out financially unless you plan to spend a lot of money doing that the rest of your life. Hold them responsible for money-making decisions early and equip them to succeed in this area.

3. Encourage Saving and Giving

I've mentioned this point before because it is essential in money training. If it's not handled well, you produce attitudes of irresponsible spending or miserly hoarding of money. The goal is to develop children who are wise with money. Every minute of training will have a positive impact on the future of their money and money management skills. There are several good resources to teach money management skills to your children. Focus on the Family has a list of such resources that you can obtain by calling (719)-531-3400.

4. Teach Children the Way Money Works by Showing Them How Bills Are Paid, How Much Things Cost, and What Kind of Budget You Use

Instead of just paying the bills, your children need to know what bills you are paying and where the money goes. It is a powerful education for young people who want cars to finally understand that in addition to the car payment, they must pay for insurance, gas, and repairs. Most never stop to think of the expense and responsibility unless you take the time to tell them.

Money as a Family Affair

In addition to the car, let them know where your money goes, so they get a feel for what percentage is being paid for taxes, basic needs, and entertainment. This adjusts their expectations of what it takes to make it.

I remember the shock and horror when I first discovered how little of my paycheck was mine to keep. Of course, I already had it spent before I got it. Until I opened it up, I had no idea there was anything called net or gross. That was a painful lesson that examining one paycheck of my father's would have eliminated.

You can make your children money wise if you stop and think and teach them what you know. Don't take for granted that they will pick up this knowledge somewhere. Allow them to pick it up from you.

5. Encourage Part-Time and Temporary Summer Jobs

Nowadays there are a lot of thirty- and forty-year-olds still living at home with Mom and Dad. They say they are looking for their niches. In reality, they never learned to work. They are lazy or afraid and would rather depend on Mom and Dad than get out there and get busy. The earlier you can free your children to get out and make their own money, the quicker the work ethic will be ingrained within them.

One of my good friends doesn't make a lot of money, but he is a master at money management. He and his wife bought an automatic breadmaker for their son, expecting to be paid back fully. The boy went door-to-door asking the neighbors if they would sign up to buy a loaf of fresh bread from him every week. He was able to sign up enough to pay back the parents and make a nice living for himself at the ripe old age of six. These kinds of ingenious ideas teach kids responsibility and good money management early in life.

6. Discuss How College Will Be Paid For

Set the expectation for college early, and discuss how you plan to finance it. You shouldn't feel guilty if you are unable to pay for all of it, but be sure your children are aware of that very early on. Don't let them take the cost of their education lightly. Help them develop at least three scenarios. One scenario might be attending a local college that is so inexpensive that if they decide to attend, you will pay for all of it. The second scenario might be a mid-range college for which you would be able to pay three-fourths. The third would be a top-level college for which you could only pay one-half the tuition.

Help your children see how they could save and invest to be able to afford the scenario of their choice. Additionally, be sure you are spending and investing your money as wisely as possible so you can give your children as much freedom as possible to attend school. In other words, don't just save for your retirement; also save for their education.

7. Steer Your Children into Thinking About Career Possibilities

I remember thinking that if I could find a career that paid one thousand dollars a month, I would have enough money for a house, a boat, and a car. Actually, that might have been true some thirty years ago when I thought it.

Be sure your kids are realistic about the career chosen. Make sure they understand the income potential of any jobs that interest them. I often talk to bright young women who want to be nurses. Nursing is a noble profession, and I have been influenced by some wonderful men and women who had nursing careers. Even with that, I would always caution anyone about going into nursing. Why? Most of the people who are in the profession are as bright as the doctors but make one-tenth the money. My suggestion is to fully explore the possibility of becoming a doctor before deciding that nursing is the right job.

The same principle applies to the lowly paid paralegal. Many who settle for this job, which is a good one and an interesting one, could have gone to a law school and gotten a law degree just as easily and made ten times the money.

Be sure your kids are realistic about their career decisions and the direction they are headed before it is too late to detour them onto what might be a more rewarding path. A final word of caution: money isn't everything, so honor children who choose a lower paying profession such as teaching because they care more about what they give than what they get financially out of their jobs.

MONEY IS NOT LOVE

Ever hear a workaholic tell a distraught spouse, "I'm doing it all for you"? I have. People are blind if they think a paycheck can replace love. Your spouse needs emotional needs met, and if you don't meet them because you are so busy making money, someone will come along who will be more than willing to meet those needs. If you neglect the legitimate needs of your spouse, be careful that while you are out making your fortune, you aren't losing the love of your life. The following story is a common one in families where bringing home the bacon takes precedence over meeting a spouse's needs.

Stan owns a chain of retail stores, and he has made millions of dollars as a merchant. He lives, eats, and breathes his work. He subscribes to every financial publication imaginable. He gets to work at 7:00 A.M. and leaves at 9:30 P.M. He has a cellular phone in his pocket and a fax machine in his car. His employees jump when he says jump, and his profits increase every fiscal year.

Stan and his wife, Carla, have two huge houses, a ski

boat, five vehicles, and a motor home. They take a trip to Europe every summer and to Hawaii every winter. In other words, by the world's standards, they have it all. Carla, in her mid-forties, has a picture-perfect life, at least on the outside. She has a designer wardrobe, a Jaguar convertible, and a credit card she can use for anything, anywhere, anytime she wants it.

The part that isn't so perfect is the affairs Carla has been having. The pattern has gone on for a decade. She has had relationships with three unlikely people, all of them not-very-successful men who took advantage of her sexually and financially. She's been emotionally burned three times, and yet she's still looking. Of course, Stan knows nothing about any of it.

Stan has invested his life in being successful and wealthy. He has given Carla everything he thought she needed. Indeed, there's only been one thing missing in her life: love. Stan has never taken the time to talk to Carla about herself, her interests, or her dreams. He's dressed her up, taken her out, and treated her like a prop on the stage setting of his life. He has never really known her at all. Unfortunately, several other men have gotten to know her quite well. Carla has been looking for love in all the wrong places for years.

Are you putting all your energy into investing financially and forgetting about your love investments? Compare the long-term benefits of a satisfying relationship with the short-term satisfaction of bolstering your own ego at the expense of the person you love. Are you possibly afraid of intimacy, and you use your business and busyness to avoid real intimacy? If you are obsessed with your work to the detriment of your marriage and don't know why, one of the best investments you will ever make is to find out why. Then you can learn to make the investments of love that will pay significant dividends for generations to come.

Sometimes writers talk about investments being made

into an "emotional bank." In *His Needs, Her Needs,* Willard F. Harley writes, "Figuratively speaking, I believe each of us has a Love Bank. It contains many different accounts, one for each person we know. Each person either makes deposits or withdrawals whenever we interact with him or her. Pleasurable interactions cause deposits, and painful interactions cause withdrawals."

The emotional bank pays back interest for a lifetime, and it isn't subject to inflation or recession. It is, however, subject to emotional bankruptcy when no deposits are made and too many withdrawals are required.

Deposits into your spouse's emotional account involve such things as meeting a woman's or man's most basic needs in marriage. Harley lists these needs of a woman:

- Caring
- Understanding
- Respect
- Devotion
- Validation
- Reassurance

A man has somewhat different needs:

- Trust
- Acceptance
- Appreciation
- Admiration
- Approval
- Encouragement

The family must never be taken for granted. They will not forgive you for forgetting them while you built monuments to yourself.

Summary:
Eight Tips for Avoiding Family Fights
over Money

1. Know your spouse's financial personality as well as your own.
2. Keep checking, savings, investments, and credit cards in joint accounts.
3. Keep all debt below 35 percent of your gross income.
4. Agree on and plan for joint financial goals.
5. Have periodic, scheduled summit meetings about family finances.
6. Agree on a budget and work together on keeping it.
7. Don't commit family money to an investment or a debt without consulting your spouse.
8. Invest in things that make both of you feel comfortable.

Seven Ways to Instill Good Financial Character
in Kids

1. Set a good example.
2. Provide a regular allowance.
3. Encourage saving and giving.
4. Teach children the way money works by showing them how bills are paid, how much things cost, and what kind of budget you use.
5. Encourage part-time and temporary summer jobs.
6. Discuss how college will be paid for.
7. Steer your children into talking about career possibilites.

CHAPTER ELEVEN

Don't Mortgage Your
Family

When Luther Jackson's funeral procession passed through the community, it created a major traffic jam. Scores of sleek luxury cars carried hundreds of mourners to the burial site. The local press was well represented, along with the *Wall Street Journal* and several other financial publications. Luther had lived big, and he was dying big. I think he would have been extremely proud of the attention he was getting. It's too bad he couldn't experience what he had worked all of his life toward.

Services were held in an exclusive chapel, which was lavishly decorated with the most elegant floral arrangements imaginable. A distinguished pastor, who didn't actually know Mr. Jackson personally, delivered a sermon that extolled the older financier's generosity and kindness to his employees and associates. There was a considerable amount of sniffling in various parts of the crowd as a well-paid soloist sang two of the popular civic leader's favorite songs.

It was not possible for the many people gathered in the chapel to see behind the curtain into the family room. They would have been surprised to know that only two people were seated there: Mr. Jackson's dry-eyed, well-dressed young wife, and an older servant who had worked for him for many years around the home. Of his four children, not one of them was present. None of his fifteen grandchildren was there, either. The ex-wife, who had mothered his sons and daughters, had chosen not to attend. Her bitterness over her husband's second marriage was far more compelling to her than any grief she might have felt over his death. And the sons and daughters had better things to do than show up to honor the man who they felt had ignored them all their lives.

Luther Jackson was a highly successful man in the business world, and his absence immediately created a huge void in the leadership of the state's economic community. At home, he was a loser. A failure. A disgrace. He had gained the whole world and lost his family—perhaps his own soul.

REMEMBERING A NOBLE FATHER

Compare Luther Jackson's funeral with my father's. My father died of a sudden heart attack while I was working on this book. His funeral served as a poignant illustration of a man who did not mortgage his family. There were so many flowers that they had to open up another room at the funeral home to accommodate them. A few were from business associates, but most were from people who loved him and loved his family. The church was packed, and the choir was full. People wept because they would miss the man who always had a joke and a smile for anyone he met. Every family member was there, all the brothers, his mother, children, and grandchildren, all willing to carry on the heritage he had left behind.

The void he left was not one in the business world, although he had many successful ventures. The void was felt in the church where young men made commitments to follow up on the projects he started. The void was in his family where his greatness was not fully realized until after he was gone. The procession was long, but it was full of people who loved him personally, not just professionally. The only regret of those in attendance was that there was not more time with my dad.

My dad invested in his family wisely. He coached Little League. He pulled us behind a ski rope for hours and hours at the lake. He was there. He was there with integrity. I am proud that he passed on to me virtues and values that have helped me succeed. Developing and nurturing relationships and doing the right thing were more important to him than having lots of money. God, his family, and his reputation led him to turn down lucrative offers in order to be a man of honor. He chose what was right over what might have made him look or feel good. Our family never took a backseat. As every life does, when examined, his life demonstrated the true values he held. The life he lived demonstrated to the people he loved that they had great value.

Any price you pay that forces your family to take a backseat is too high a price. Many breadwinners say, "I proved I loved you by providing for you," when their loved ones ask why they demonstrated so little love on a daily basis in the home. People on their deathbeds regret too little time with the family, not the desire for having had more profit, prestige, or power. Getting by with a little less can make most people a lot happier and more financially secure. A lot of people took huge risks financially during the 1980s. But today, it's not so tempting as it was then. As one sociologist put it, when people make extravagant investments today, "they get the wind kicked out of them."

Naturally, wise financial decisions on behalf of the family are necessary. Unlike what Luther Jackson did, it is possible to devote a reasonable amount of time to providing well for your spouse and children without abandoning them in the process. Like anything else in life, this requires balance—enough interest in money to make good choices, but not such an obsession with wealth that all else is secondary.

You can check yourself to see if you are covering the basics:

- Do you take at least one day of rest each week to relax with your family?
- Do you take vacations (without being consumed with business-related thoughts and actions)?
- Are the special events (sports, school plays, field trips) of your family members on your agenda?
- Do you have undistracted time alone with your spouse each week?

You may feel that you are trapped in a situation where you want to spend more time with your family, but you are not in a position to do so because of financial demands. You may have gotten behind financially, and you are furiously trying to catch up in hopes of the day when you will have enough time with your family. One couple I know are in this situation. A family crisis put both out of work several years ago. But both are working now. The husband took a job in restaurant management. His hours are irregular with mostly late-night shifts. This shift work causes him to miss out on time with their three young children who are in day care during the day when he is home. He hates the toll his job is taking on his family, but he doesn't see a way out because of financial limitations.

Don't Mortgage Your Family

If financial limitations are keeping you from having the kind of relationship you truly want with your family, my advice to you is the advice I gave my friends: plan for a way out. It may take you several years to get the education or other skills necessary to change career fields, but start now to make a transition. Creatively consider your options as a team, and plan how you can have a career that does not mortgage your family. Explain your plan to your children so they know that you are working because you love them and that you are preparing to make changes that will give you more time with them. If this is your situation, use your desire to have more time with your family as motivation to implement the principles in this book. Learning to manage your money well can free you to have the time and energy your family needs from you.

The wise professional invests in family first. Their needs are the priority, and once those are met, then the person is ready to make financial investments. It is a matter of priority and honor.

To be an honorable professional, you cannot make it all in business and then destroy it all at home. Ensure that your first investment is a family investment that will reap many more rewards than an investment or a job that has ten times the returns of the original money.

FAMILY MONEY

It's important for you to keep yourself well informed about where the family money is going. After consulting with experts in the field of finance, I've learned that average American families spend their money something like this:

- Housing—32 percent
- Transportation—17.4 percent
- Finances (credit, etc.)—14.8 percent

- Food—14.4 percent
- Clothing—5.9 percent
- Health care—5.2 percent
- Entertainment—5 percent
- Education—1.5 percent
- Other—3.8 percent

When I first read this list, I saw it as a reflection of a family that is self-obsessed. The lack of money being allocated to give to great causes or the church struck me as a sign of selfishness. I've been raised with the understanding that a budget is not complete unless a portion is set aside to save and give. However, this approach is not typical of the American family.

While discussing this subject with a friend, she offered another perspective. She suggested that perhaps the cause is not self-obsession, at least not in the sense of selfishness to the neglect of others. Perhaps their lack of giving and saving is due to feelings of deprivation, believing they will never have enough, and so the thought of giving seems out of reach.

As demonstrated by the people living in poverty in the village in India I told you about earlier, you are never so poor that you cannot give something. Perhaps there is fear, ignorance, or a lack of money management skills. Whatever the case, these shortsighted attitudes rob a family of one of the greatest sources of joy available: the joy of giving.

Sandy and I usually try to give anonymously or at least not draw attention to our giving. However, for the sake of encouraging you to find the joy and satisfaction of giving, I will share two incidents from our family life. My brother Jerry died of AIDS. He came home to die, and our family and the community were wonderful in the way they accepted him and comforted him at the end of his life. In dealing with the pain of losing my brother and the shame associated with AIDS, I saw how many people die a lonely death, being rejected by family and friends. We decided that one of the best ways we could demonstrate the love of God would be to comfort people with AIDS. Therefore, we gave time and money to set up a hospice for people with AIDS.

In another instance, my wife, Sandy, has a friend whose daughter is chronically ill. Their family had only one car, used by the husband to drive to and from work. Sandy's friend was often left home with a sick child with no way to transport her for medical appointments and emergencies. Sandy and a group of her friends decided to buy the woman a second car. They pooled their resources and bought a Honda Accord. They took the woman out to lunch and afterward surprised her with the keys to her car. Words cannot adequately express the sense of joy felt by that group as they watched their friend drive away in tears. We have owned some nice cars over the years. However, the greatest excitement we have known in buying a car came from participating in the purchase of that Honda for someone who needed it.

Regardless of your income or level of debt, I encourage you to adjust your percentages based on your values and the legacy you would like to leave behind. The money that will mean most to a family is the money that will be given away and invested in making the world a better place in which to live.

FAMILY FIRST, FINANCES SECOND

When you have taken care of setting your priority on the family, it is time to consider how to invest and what to do to ensure that along with emotional security, there is financial security for the family. Perhaps the best place to look first to ensure financial security is at credit. In conversations with family budget consultants, I've discovered that:

WINNING AT WORK

- Sixty percent of people have borrowed more money than can be paid for in a lifetime. Because of credit abuse, when these people die, relatives will be left holding the bag, but it will be an empty bag with a hole in it. More than half of American families are struggling just to get by, even though on average we make more than most people in most every other country.

- Forty percent must borrow to pay off money already borrowed. Using a home credit line has become an epidemic for those who are sick with credititis. They take the money out of equity built up in the house, pay down the mortgage, and then run the credit cards right back up to where they were. All they did was increase the amount of junk they had and double their debt. Don't give in to the temptation of paying something off only to build back a stack of additional credit card debt.

- The best investment you can make is to pay off high-interest debt. Paying off an 18 percent loan is the equivalent of investing with an 18 percent return. Furthermore, although you're taxed on an investment, money you save by paying early is tax-free. It is hard for many to understand or think in these terms, partly because lenders make money when you keep yourself in debt; therefore, advertising encourages consumer debt. This is a simple concept. If I have $100 at 18 percent interest, that's 18 percent interest out of my pocket to borrow the money; when I pay it off, it is putting 18 percent back into my pocket. It is hard to find a way to spend $100 that would put 18 percent back in your pocket. Paying off credit card debt is one of them, however.

Don't Mortgage Your Family

Begin your financial planning at the point of your credit cards. What good will it do if you invest $100 while you spend another $200 you didn't really need to spend? If your spending were under control, if the impulses to spend were deadened, you would end up with $300, not just the $100. To get this area under control, you may have to cut up your credit cards.

My wife and I did it, and it made all the difference in the world in how much money we now have left after we pay the bills. We used to have several cards from major retail chains in addition to bank cards. Our spending regularly got out of hand. Now we keep only one bank card for use when necessary and commit to pay the balance by the end of each month.

One compulsive spender could not bear to cut up her credit cards. She keeps them on ice—literally. She freezes her cards in a container of water. When she really wants to use a credit card, she takes one out to thaw. This process forces her to take time to consider if the purchase is worth the weight of debt.

Living without credit cards after you have grown accustomed to using them means adapting to a new way of life. You must first calculate your regular expenses, the ones you typically find on your budget: regularly scheduled bills, household expenses, monthly payments, and so on. Then you must calculate the expenses most people overlook, the expenses that show up every year: car registration, school photos, car repairs, club dues, and any other expenses that require money but aren't on a regular schedule. Make it a goal to have one savings account you don't touch and another savings account connected to your regular checking account. You need to build up a reserve in this secondary account to be used for miscellaneous expenses that you used to put on your credit card.

Once you make this switch, at the end of the year, reward yourself tangibly by doing something fun for the family with some of the money you would have otherwise spent on finance charges.

You may need help keeping accurate accounts of your personal finances. I strongly encourage you to learn to use a money management computer program. Even if you are computer illiterate, I see this help as so valuable it would be worth buying a personal computer and taking a class just to be able to manage your finances so simply. Anyone can learn to use one of these programs, and it makes a world of difference in managing your money.

SIX INVESTMENT RESOLUTIONS

Once you have managed your credit issues well, you are ready to look at investing money for your future. You may want to start by investing the money you would have thrown away in finance charges. Then you really have nothing to lose! When you feel you're ready to invest, don't allow yourself to be impulsive. Do your homework; talk to qualified and experienced people. And take into consideration the following resolutions I recommend.

1. Before I Invest One Cent in Anything, I Will Learn Its Risks as Well as Its Potential Rewards

I don't do that just to avoid risk; I also do it to insure there is some. There must be some risk if you are to gain rewards. If you are too conservative, you will miss out on many opportunities to earn more money on your money. Having watched a mutual fund do nothing but sit there, never earning anything, I understand the perils of too little risk.

I also understand the problems with too much risk, having directed a lot of money into foreign stocks just before they fell. Of course, that was before I decided to allow someone else to manage my investments, a decision that cost a little but reaped many more rewards than it cost.

Don't Mortgage Your Family

It is time to let someone else manage your investments anytime you have $30,000 or more to invest (unless you have a few hours a day to devote to managing your investments personally). Over the course of twenty years, $30,000 can turn into $2 million if it is managed with good judgment. Therefore, don't try to save yourself management fees in the short run that will cost you big bucks in the long run.

2. I Will Have a Diversified Portfolio: Short-Term, Intermediate-Term, Stocks or Bonds, and Real Estate

It didn't happen overnight, but I eventually spread the investments around so that no matter what happens to the economy, some investment I have can benefit from it. If I had done this before the overseas fiasco, retirement would be a lot closer than it is.

3. I Will Avoid Once-in-a-Lifetime Opportunities

My wife and I started a swimwear company with dreams that it was a once-in-a-lifetime opportunity. We got some nice deductions some years and made money others, but no dreams ever really came true. If we had taken the money we put into it and invested that money much more conservatively, we would have gotten a greater reward. Fortunately for us, all money invested came back to us. Most once-in-a-lifetime opportunities turn into great losses that cannot be overturned.

4. I Will Not Allow the Fear of Taxes to Determine My Investment Choices

A man suggested to me that I not do something that would net me $500,000 because of the taxes I would have to pay on that amount. Until the tax rate is 100 percent, it is always better to make money than not make it. The real key is to not make an investment in order to get tax relief. That could be reversed or go away by the time you cash in the investment. Make investments that will make you money rather than save you on taxes.

5. I Will Set a Target Price for My Stocks, so I'll Know When It's Time to Sell

I do this at the top and the bottom of the spectrum. It is very hard to cut your losses or to think that your stock won't continue to make a lot of money. Use good counsel on when it is right to get out of an investment.

I have a friend who went in on a four-way deal on a condo in Maui. He and his wife paid $10,000 down, and they have to pay $200 a month and $49 a night when they want to use it. It has gone down in value rather than up. They stay there ten days a year. He is putting almost $3,000 a year into a place that he could be spending vacationing anywhere in the world. Or he could invest it in something that would produce a nice return. The problem is, he doesn't want to give up the $10,000 he invested.

Consider the cost of that money by comparing what would have happened if he had earned 10 percent a year for ten years. Also consider that at around $3,000 a year into the property, he would almost have his $10,000 back in three years. He would in that length of time if he wisely invested the money he saved. Don't get caught in his trap. Be willing to cut your losses and go on to the next opportunity. Don't throw good money after bad.

6. I Will Evaluate My Portfolio Every Month

My portfolio is on my computer, and it updates itself. If you can possibly afford an on-line service, it is a nice way to keep track of how you are doing. Keeping track today may land you an extra $10,000 in ten years, so don't neglect your future.

There are several major reasons for taking control of your money to invest it and spend it wisely. The reasons correlate to the most common and realistic fears people have when it comes to money. Here are the big ones that motivate me to spend less and invest more:

- Losing control of credit card or other debt
- Running up a medical bill too big to pay
- Being unable to purchase a home
- Being unable to finance the children's college education
- Not having the ability to afford a comfortable retirement

Any one of these should be enough to motivate you to get your financial act together for yourself and your family and your future. Family and finances are always tough to balance, but you can do it with a little effort and planning. Involving your family will make all that you do much more rewarding.

Summary:
Six Investment Resolutions

1. Before investing one cent in anything, learn its risks as well as its potential rewards.
2. Have a diversified portfolio.
3. Avoid once-in-a-lifetime opportunities.
4. Don't allow the fear of taxes to determine your investment choices.
5. Set a target price for your stocks so you'll know when it's time to sell.
6. Evaluate your portfolio every month.

CHAPTER TWELVE

Countering the Greed Factor

I n his book *True Freedom,* psychiatrist Verle Bell writes,

> I define "greed" as our drivenness, our insatiable hunger, our desperate attempts to gain all sorts of things that in the possessing will make us feel valuable, strong and secure. I believe our greed can be overcome by a new way of thinking. We need to form new goals, new hopes. We need to start reminding ourselves of the following truth: I cannot secure my future but God already has so I can rest in his finished work.

It's true. Greed is more than an unhealthy craving for more and more money and possessions. It is an inner hunger that seeks control and power. Greed looks for the quick fix and the instant solution. It tries to assure us that we'll be set for life and have nothing to worry about. It soon becomes a state of living for money and possessions.

Greedy people don't really have a money problem; they have a faith problem. People with the faith that God will provide for their needs will see no reason to work an eighty-hour week. In fact, people with faith would come to believe that the money made from sacrificing family time would be the money that would end up causing all of the future problems. Certainly, we can see the problems that come out of homes where parents have abandoned the family to go off and earn more money than would ever be needed to live comfortably. The money itself can actually be the source of future problems, involving the person in deals that never should have been struck and/or partnerships formed.

GETTING RID OF GREED

There are some steps that you can take to rid yourself of greedy thoughts and behaviors. Here is a good place to begin with getting the greed out of your life.

1. Relinquish Control of Your Possessions

Greedy people hold on to their possessions much too tightly. They feel the only hope is to maintain 100 percent control of every dollar spent. Many are so caught up in withholding possessions that they will miss out on a whole dimension of life.

One of the greatest joys of life is reaching a point where you can give up control of your possessions and allow God to take over what you really don't have control of anyway. Ask for God's help in allocating to you just the right amount of money to take care of all of your needs and a healthy portion of your desires. If you have funds left over after that, ask God how you should give it away to mean the most and help the most people.

2. Simplify Your Lifestyle

I think most people are amazed at just how empty an extravagant lifestyle is. The more they spend and the more they make, the emptier they feel. Those who seek fulfillment eliminate the greed and simplify rather than magnify their lifestyles. Like the now deceased Sam Walton of Wal-Mart did, they may still drive the same old truck or live in the same house in order to keep their feet firmly planted in reality.

Most people who get a large chunk of money make a horrible mistake when they get it. They take it and buy something that increases their cost of living. Then they need even more money to break even. The best and most prevalent example is a boat. People get money, buy a boat, and then almost literally are throwing money down a hole from the expense of operation and upkeep. Now they really have to make some money because their cost of living has risen so much. Simplification stops the drive for more and more and reduces greedy impulses.

When making any purchase, be sure to accurately consider the unspoken commitment you are making to ongoing future expenses. To do this, don't just take the word of the sales representative. Find others who made a similar purchase over a year ago. Ask them to tell you the upside and downside of additional responsibilities and expenses that come with the purchase. If you are not willing and able to make that kind of commitment, resist the urge to buy.

3. Control Your Spending

Until you bring your spending under control, you will always be driven to get more and more. Someone whose spending is out of control, emotionally motivated, and self-indulgent can be likened to a promiscuous person. The issues that need to be addressed may be similar. Or you may be fiscally and sexually promiscuous, using the same kind of motivation and justification to lead you into self-indulgence. Just as those who lose control of emotions and cross moral boundaries need to be held accountable to someone who knows their intimate secrets, those who lose control of spending need someone to hold them accountable for what they spend and how they spend it.

At the Minirth Meier New Life Clinics, we have programs for addictive-compulsive behavior. People who come in for treatment for sex addiction often find their promiscuity has broadened into many areas of life. There are also those who come in just because their spending is compulsively out of control. Fiscal promiscuity can destroy a marriage, too. If you or someone you love is dealing with issues related to compulsive spending, help is available and should be sought.

4. Learn Gratitude and Contentment

There is nothing like an attitude change to bring greed under control if you have a wandering eye that continues to roam and lose focus because it is always looking at someone who has more or at least looks more successful than you. Rather than compare, be grateful for what you have, and learn to be content with a lot or a little.

Many people forget that the Ten Commandments include this command: thou shalt not covet. Many don't know what coveting is or may see it as part of the American way of life. Coveting is looking at something others have with longing that causes you to envy them and desire what they have as your own. Covetousness causes chronic dissatisfaction with life, regardless of your economic level.

Check yourself for covetousness, and make corrections if you find it. Ask yourself,

- Do I find myself dissatisfied with what I have because I compare it to what others have?
- Who do I envy, and why?

All of us want to be in control. Many think that money allows them to have that control. They don't realize that they are driven and propelled by their greed. In that case they do not control the money; the money controls them. If the greed doesn't get resolved, it can drive them to ruin. If you have it, do what you need to do to turn greed into gratitude and contentment.

MAKING ENDS MEET

The more often you find a way to make ends meet, the less greed for more will drive you. All of us find it difficult at times to make ends meet. And our desire to have enough may feel a little like greed when we focus our attention on it. Instead of fixating on how to get more money in the wallet, think about these five ways of making cash last until the end of the month.

1. Track Down Every Dollar You Spend

I don't recommend becoming obsessive about your spending, but I do think that it can be helpful to do a one-time study of every dollar you spend. Keep a log of every dollar you spend for one month; then add your checks and credit card purchases and see where all the money has gone. Most people who do this are shocked at how much is thrown away on fast food or clothes or some other category that they never dreamed could consume so much.

Once you find out where you are wasting the most money, you can act to bring that area under control. Computer money management systems make this process easy. All you do is categorize your spending when you pay bills by

Countering the Greed Factor

computer or input your spending information. Then the computer keeps track of where every penny goes and creates reports that show you how you spend your money.

Earlier I mentioned an old-fashioned envelope system for allocating how much money to spend in each category. This system can be cumbersome and impractical, but if you take the two categories that are most out of control and then allocate the money you want to spend into envelopes, it could become the key to getting your finances back in order. All it requires is determining how much you can spend in that category and putting that much in the envelope. When you run out of money, don't spend anymore in that category. Eventually, you will become accustomed to the lower amount, and you won't need to use the envelopes anymore.

2. Don't Carry Around Too Much Cash

I love to hear stories of wealthy people who have to borrow a quarter to make a phone call because they do not carry money around with them. Those of us who have less tend to carry much more than we need. It doesn't burn a hole in our pockets; it flies out of our pockets and into the pockets of others.

3. Avoid Paying Top Dollar When You Don't Need to Do So

Shop at outlets and discount warehouses instead of chic retail stores. My wife and I have a lot of fun shopping at outlets and finding bargains at the club and warehouse stores. Today more than ever it is easier to find good quality clothes at very reasonable prices. The only thing you have to be willing to do is wear it about six months later than a few other people who paid top dollar for it.

4. Before You Travel, Research Discounted Airfares and Hotel Accommodations

One of the ways our finances creep away from us is in the form of travel expenses. If you examine some people's finances, you find that they do a great job of living within their means except for the three trips they can't afford that year. They literally vacation themselves into debt. If you find yourself in that situation, plan ahead soon enough and do enough research that you can get the best buys. Most people can travel for one-third of what they are spending if they look for the right bargains.

Call your travel agent to plan ahead with bargains in mind. If you don't have your heart set on a specific destination but are looking for R&R, ask your agent to suggest destinations with reduced costs. You may also want to plan and pay for your vacation with cash up front. If you are putting everything on a credit card as you travel, to be dealt with when the vacation is over, you are likely to spend far more than if you plan a travel budget in advance and pay cash. You will be far more conservative that way.

5. Shop Around to Find Sales and Bargains

Just changing the time of the season you shop can result in significant savings. Look at end-of-season sales as a way to save money. For example, if you make a practice of buying Christmas decorations, wrap, and cards the week after Christmas to be saved for next year, you will save over 50 percent. Buying produce at farmers' markets will ensure that you get the freshest produce and you will get it at a considerable discount over grocery store prices. If you plan ahead with sales in mind, you can save big.

Countering the Greed Factor

ECONOMIC WORRIES

Another reason we get greedy other than spending too much is that we may be experiencing fears about an economy that is both tough and untrustworthy. We worry about not having enough money, and we worry even more about losing our jobs. It's not a bad idea to think about the worst-case scenario once in a while.

Here are seven rules for survival in a difficult economy.

1. Keep Your Eyes Open

Know what jobs in your field are available in case you have to make a sudden move. The average worker in our economy will change jobs at least seven times in the course of a working life. Have a basic resume ready at all times. When things look uncertain where you are, remember that even in the worst economic times there are those who will do well. Prepare to be one of them. Break down your skills in such a way that you can show how those skills could be applicable in various situations.

Don't panic. If you do have to change jobs unexpectedly, your advance preparation will give you a head start over your competitors.

2. Be More Concerned About Pay Than Perks

If you are offered a job where perks (for example, a company car, club membership, first-class seats and accommodations) are part of the package, negotiate for more money and fewer perks. The cash in your pocket gives you the option of using the money to add to your financial security, to invest wisely. Or if you so choose, you can opt for some of the perks along the way.

3. Don't Be a Snob

A discount store may not offer your dream job, but it could provide a lot better future than a designer boutique. During times of economic uncertainty, opt for a company that is providing a good service at fair prices. These companies will do well in uncertain times. When the economy is more stable and your personal finances allow you to take more of a risk, you can opt to seek employment with a company that may be here one day and gone the next.

4. Beware of Working for Small Independent Companies

Compared to a large corporation, a small independent has a higher rate of turnover, and the chance of the company's going belly-up is more likely. More autonomy doesn't necessarily mean more job security. Do your homework to find out the history of the company and the people running it. If their history gives you reason to believe their future is secure, go for it. However, be more careful than you would otherwise be when dealing with an established firm that employs many people.

5. Think Globally

You may find your future in another part of the world. The global village theorized a few decades ago is where we live today. There is no reason to limit yourself to national boundaries or even boundaries between continents. Thanks to the development of a global communication network, the sky isn't the limit anymore. The messages we send up to the sky bounce around the world, thanks to satellite communication. You don't even need to move. With the information highway you can stay home and provide services around the globe. Rethink what you have to offer in light of needs around the world. Then find a need and fill it.

Countering the Greed Factor

6. Whenever Possible, Work Under Contract

Working under contract affords many advantages to working for a salary. When you do so, more of your expenses are tax deductible. You also have the advantage of being able to put more of your savings (15 percent up to $30,000 per year) in a tax-deferred self-employment plan. This has significant advantages over a 401(K) or a traditional IRA. Working under contract also allows you to be more in command of your time and resources, which you can use to your advantage whether at work or at home.

7. Keep Records of Your Best Efforts

Keep a file for commendations, memos of praise, incidents of recognition, and details of success. Anytime someone writes something positive about you or your work, keep it for future reference. If you are in a sales-related job, make it part of your work to make the most of these commendations. Anytime someone gives you a compliment about your work, ask him whether he would mind your using the comments to inform others about the quality of your work. Write the comments he made about you in a letter. Ask him to read it, and if it reflects his genuine opinion of your work, ask him to sign it so you can share it with other prospective customers. He may even be willing to copy it onto the company letterhead. As your file of commendations grows, so does your job security. Employers are always impressed with a worker who comes highly recommended.

Some people react to uncertain economic times by becoming more greedy. They act as though there is only so much to go around, and they are going to make sure they get the biggest slice of the pie. The truth is, there is no set amount of prosperity to go around. People create economic security and even wealth by wise responses in all economic climates. Don't let the state of the economy become an excuse for greed.

Greed is squelched when we spend less, become grateful for what we have, and prepare for the worst that could happen to us economically. If you suffer from greed, more than enough will never be enough. You will exhaust yourself and your family looking for the satisfaction that can never come from money. Become willing to do whatever it takes to eliminate the greed factor from your life.

Summary:
Getting Rid of Greed

1. Relinquish control of your possessions.
2. Simplify your lifestyle.
3. Control your spending.
4. Learn gratitude and commitment.

Five Ways to Make Cash Last until the End of the Month

1. Track down every dollar you spend.
2. Don't carry around too much cash.
3. Avoid paying top dollar when you don't need to do so.
4. Before you travel, research discounted airfares and hotel accommodations.
5. Shop around to find sales and bargains.

Seven Rules for Survival in a Difficult Economy

1. Keep your eyes open.
2. Be more concerned with pay than perks.
3. Don't be a snob.
4. Beware of working for small, independent companies.
5. Think globally.
6. Whenever possible, work under contract.
7. Keep records of your best efforts.

Part 4

The Meaning

CHAPTER THIRTEEN

Looking for Meaning with the Right Perspective

We've talked about the mission. We've looked at both sides of the money coin. Now let's contemplate that third element—meaning. What exactly do I mean by meaning? Appreciation of life's pleasures is nothing new. Around 300 B.C. Epicurus said,

> It is impossible to live pleasurably
> without living wisely, well, and justly,
> and impossible to live wisely, well, and justly without
> living pleasurably.

Some things never change, and Epicurus's words are an ancient Greek way of saying that we have to keep the mission and the money in balance with the meaning. When I talk about meaning, I'm referring to the pleasures and emotional rewards of life such as the following:

- Leisure time activities
- Positive relationships
- Professional honors
- Enjoyment of the arts
- Appreciation of beauty
- Children's accomplishments
- Philosophical reflection
- Spiritual devotion
- Moments of joy

Where do these experiences fit into your plans? Are you imbalanced, centering your world on them or forgetting about them altogether?

The meaning also refers to the rewards of a job well done. Some call this the psychic rewards of work (not to be confused with anything that has to do with the Psychic Friends Network). Meaning for me comes when I participate in a seminar and someone reveals a painful secret never shared with another human being. Meaning comes into play when I take time to tell a hotel clerk that everything about the stay went well. I experience a simple element of joy when I see the smile appear on the face at receiving the compliment and see the sagging shoulders lift. Meaning comes from the pleasure we derive when we produce a product as well as that product can be produced. If you are not allowing the meaning of your work to guide you and motivate you, you probably would do better in another job.

IMPROVE YOUR PERSPECTIVE

We may tend to get caught up in all that we do and lose sight of all that is truly important. We get so focused on the business that we forget who we are and why we are here. Sometimes it helps to stop and do an exercise or two that can help us get a new or fresh perspective on the meaning of our lives and where work should be fitting rather than where it actually does fit.

Most of us don't keep track of the successes and failures of anyone but ourselves. We may cast an envious or admiring glance at others from time to time, but rarely do we remember the key things about their lives. See if you can answer the following questions.

1. Who are the seven wealthiest people in the United States?

2. What are the names of the top fifteen American corporations and their CEOs?

3. Who were the last five losing presidential candidates?

4. Who are the top ten military officers in the American armed services?

5. Who are the twelve most admired businesspeople in your community?

If you can answer all these questions, you are exceptionally well informed. But most people don't focus attention on the successes of others. We may not even take time to focus on the overall meaning of our own lives. We may be at a loss when it comes to self-evaluation. We sometimes feel we're the last to know some of the most significant things about ourselves. We get so involved in our daily schedules that we completely lose track of what we've accomplished, who we are, and where we're headed. We're surprised when people pay us huge compliments (or maybe we're surprised when they don't!). We're shocked when we catch a glimpse of ourselves in some "mirror" we encounter unexpectedly along the way.

Gaining perspective on your life is an invaluable step toward finding the balance of mission, money, and meaning. Take a few minutes, think through the following questions, and write out your answers.

TEN QUESTIONS ABOUT THE PAST

1. What are the ten most important lessons you've learned in your life?

2. Who are ten key people whose friendships have run like a thread through your life? What do they mean to you?

3. Can you discern an invisible hand at work behind the scenes of your life? In what circumstances have you most seen providential guidance or intervention?

4. What are the ten worst things that have ever happened to you? What good came out of them?

5. Which of your personal traits have served you the best in your life?

6. Which traits have caused you the most problems?

7. What was the best time of your life? Why?

8. What have been your ten most significant accomplishments?

9. Have you ever had a prayer answered? What happened?

10. If you had it all to do again, what would you do differently?

TEN QUESTIONS ABOUT THE PRESENT

1. What are the three problems or concerns that worry you the most?

2. For what ten things are you the most grateful?

3. If you could change anything in your life today, what would it be? Why haven't you changed it?

4. How would you describe your present physical health condition?

5. What small pleasures do you look forward to on a daily basis?

6. Which five people are the most positive and uplifting in your life? Why?

7. Which five people are the most draining, demanding, and difficult for you to deal with?

8. If you died today, who do you think would attend your funeral?

9. How many times a day do you pray?

10. What kinds of thoughts come to mind when you take the time for reflection or meditation? Fears? Hopes? Blessings?

TEN QUESTIONS ABOUT THE FUTURE

1. What do you think your life will be like twenty years from now?

2. Try to imagine your thoughts on your deathbed. What will you wish you'd done differently? What will you feel you've done well?

3. What is your most recurring daydream?

4. What are your five greatest fears about the future?

5. What are your five greatest hopes for the future?

6. Do you feel you have to face the future alone, or do you believe that God will walk through it with you?

7. What is the one thing you'd like to change in order to make the future better?

8. Which five people's friendship or love would you want to know you'd have for the rest of your life?

9. Have you ever committed your future into the care of God?

10. What are the ten questions you would like to ask Him?

It is never too late to start looking for meaning with the right perspective. It is never too late to begin looking at the meaningful and spiritual side of life. Doing that is for everyone—everyone who wants more than the mundane existence that comes through materialism. If you passed over all these questions and didn't answer them, I'd like to strongly urge you to go back and do something that could have a real impact on you for the rest of your life.

Summary:
Nine Pleasures and Emotional Rewards of Life

1. Schedule leisure time activities.
2. Develop positive relationships.
3. Seek professional honors.
4. Invest in enjoyment of the arts.
5. Take time for appreciation of beauty.
6. Share the joy of your children's accomplishments.
7. Take time for philosophical reflection.
8. Schedule daily spiritual devotion.
9. Learn to recognize and appreciate moments of joy.

CHAPTER FOURTEEN

The Meaning of Winning with Character

We all know of those instances where people win the battle but lose the war. The best illustration of this I've seen is in a children's book called *The Bear & The Fly*, a story by Paula Winter. The story is told without words, but the pictures really do say it all. The opening scene shows a family of bears eating dinner with their little dog at their feet. Then a fly buzzes in the open window. Papa Bear gets the fly swatter and attempts to swat the fly as his wife and daughter look on. He succeeds in knocking the food and drink off the table.

His determination grows. In his second attempt to swat the fly, he hits Mama Bear on the head. She is knocked out at the table while the fly buzzes around Daughter Bear's head. Papa takes aim again . . . SWAT! Daughter Bear is unconscious on the floor. Papa Bear is furious. He'll get that fly if it's the last thing he does. The little dog tries to help. SWAT . . . oops! He misses the fly, but the dog is out cold.

The crazed Papa Bear will not relent. He chases the fly around the room, swatting and knocking things over. Then he puts a chair on top of the table in an attempt to reach the fly, now resting on the ceiling. The chair falls off the table, taking Papa Bear down with it.

The house is a shambles. Every member of the family is out. The dinner is ruined. The TV is broken. The fly buzzes out the open window. The original goal was realized, but somewhere along the line Papa Bear lost his sense of how his actions related to his overall goals.

People of character make a point of making sure they do not compromise the overall good or doing what is right in the process of seeking any particular goal. The point is well taken that there is no value in winning a small conflict if, in the end, you lose everything else in the process. The same holds true with winning at work. Why would you want to win at any particular facet of life, achieve any particular goal, or make money in an endeavor if it meant that it would turn you into a long-term loser? The only kind of win that means anything is the kind of win that allows you to develop and maintain your character. If you have to compromise character to win, it doesn't matter how much money you make; you are a loser.

Prisons are full of some very big-time winners. They won with junk bonds. Or they won with savings-and-loan dollars ripped out of retirement accounts of older people. They found a way to win but lost all they had because they abandoned their character. They stand for nothing because they have no backbone to hold them up. Winning without character is never winning at all.

Character is built in the dark when no one is looking or at home when no one is applauding. It is reflected in your checkbook and on your charge card bills, determining how you spend, how you invest your money, and how much you give. Character helps you be who you are in public at those times when you are completely alone. It is the act of doing things that you never regret. Character developed at home is character that wins at work. You can't just pick it up going one way or the other. You have to work on it, commit to it, and allow it to drive all of your decisions.

Winning with character is not easy. Too few people accomplish it. It starts with parents modeling it, and it manifests itself in individuals who set out to do things that make them feel right about themselves rather than good about themselves. God honors people with character and blesses them with children who carry that torch of character on to their children and grandchildren. If you find that this is an area of your life that is lacking, it is not too late to decide to make some changes in the way you live, the way you think, and the way you make and spend your money.

There are some signs that I look for in evaluating character. See if you agree that these are elements of character.

SIGNS OF GOOD CHARACTER

1. Self-Confidence

When people have a sense of self-confidence, they aren't trying to find new ways to compensate for their feelings of inferiority. They know they have some God-given strengths, and they use them appropriately. People who are involved in shady dealings are worried about being caught and found out, and they lack a sense of self-confidence. As opposed to self-obsession, self-confidence is the realistic appraisal of strengths and the utilization of them.

2. Living within Means

People without character will try to compensate by having flashy possessions and by spending themselves out of control. People with character use restraint and delayed gratification to ensure they aren't spending more than they are making. They are more interested in future security than they are in appearing to be something they are not.

3. Getting Along Well with Others

Characterless individuals will be envious of others who may do as well or better than they do. They may fear being replaced. Each person is seen as a potential threat to job security. Therefore, people without character typically pick fights and disrupt the peace. They just can't seem to get along.

4. A Positively Helpful Attitude

People with character never say that it isn't their job. They are always trying to find a new way to help others. They are encouraging, and since they carry such little emotional baggage, they find a way to be positive and see the positive in other people. They are delighted to see someone get ahead and feel that they had a part in the advancement.

5. Consideration of Others

People with good character are able to put themselves in perspective and focus on other people's needs. They don't push ahead of others; they find joy in putting others first. This consideration of others usually results in others pushing them ahead and wanting them to succeed.

6. Patience

Character allows others time to develop. There is no demand to toe the line or make the grade immediately. Their self-control and self-confidence allow them to wait for others to figure out a way to succeed. People with character are willing to trust God rather than demand that things be different.

7. Hunger for Learning

People of character show a desire to know more, do more, and be more. They seek out others who can teach them more. They read so that the mind can continue to grow. They never have the attitude that they know it all, and they continue to look for sources that will increase their knowledge.

8. Growth in Skills and Talents

People with character are always seeking new ways to grow their skills and develop their talents. They want to be better tomorrow than they are today. They are never satisfied with resting on past accomplishments and maintaining the status quo. Growth is the goal.

9. Reliability

You can always count on people with character. They are there when needed, especially when others find it too painful to be there. Character is founded in painful commitments and those with character know how to keep them.

10. Unselfishness

People with character are actually out to further the good of the organization. Their moves are not always focused on what makes them look the best or glorifies their own careers. They are a joy to work with because they are always finding a new way to make the workplace an enjoyable place to live.

The employee with good character is someone you won't have to worry about and you won't have to look over his shoulder. If someone has to look over yours, you don't have it. If you lack good character, all you are earning may be for naught in the final evaluation.

Evaluate the gray areas of your life, and determine that in the name of character you will remove the need for anyone to look over your shoulder. Tax forms, expense accounts, and money given to charity—all are indications of character or its lack. If you have it, people will notice, and you will be rewarded for it.

11. Love of People

People of good character are careful to love people and use things. They will not have a reputation as users. People enjoy being used by God, but they tend to resent being used by others and see it as a character flaw. Be careful to see if you are a person who shows the characteristics of love. The Bible says that love is patient and kind, not envious, not proud, and seeks not its own way. In seeking your own way, you might be running over others who have to yield to you out of necessity or dependence on you.

DYING WITH CHARACTER

People with character are mature enough to consider those who come after them. Character is especially important when considering what happens and what is left in the case of death. Is your family protected in case you die? Many heartsick widows have been left in financial ruin because their husbands "seized the day" and ignored the future. If you haven't looked out for your family's welfare in the event of your death, you should.

When my father died, I helped my mother with the task of sorting through the insurance policies and the benefits she had to live on. My father had been very thoughtful, and his love is sustained after his life ended. He had a pension from Texas A&M with several options. He took the option of taking less money while he was alive so my mother would have more money after he died. She will always have financial freedom, which means that my brother and I can work on taking care of our families without having to reserve a lot of money for her care. That was a great gift from my father to all of us.

The Meaning of Winning

Dad also had life insurance that provided my mother with a small nest egg for extra expenses and emergencies. If you have a family dependent on your income but don't have life insurance, think about the effect of your death on them. Immediately begin to explore the options available for life insurance. Don't comfort yourself with the thought that you are young and have plenty of time. Accidents happen every day. The day to purchase life insurance is the day others depend on you financially (that may be on your wedding day or the day your first child is born).

And once you begin to explore various policies, here are five questions to ask about life insurance:

1. What type of insurance best suits my needs?
2. How much insurance do I need, and why?
3. How financially strong is the insurer?
4. How realistic are the policy illustrations?
5. Will the premiums go up or down, and if so, how much?

At a minimum, find a term life insurance policy that you can afford, and begin paying the premiums. Term life insurance is inexpensive. It may be hard to pay out money for the policy, but character calls you to think of those who come after you. Your sacrifice today will be part of your legacy and will lend honor to your name long after you are gone.

If you find that good character is lacking in your life, it is not too late to decide to make some changes in the way you live, the way you think, and the way you spend your money. Good character brings its own rewards and is essential to winning at work without losing at love.

Let me close with a story about the obvious benefits of good character. Many years ago Pat Boone was on the "Tonight Show Starring Johnny Carson." Members of the Boone family have become American symbols of good character.

That night Pat Boone looked great, suntanned, relaxed, and healthy. Johnny Carson asked him, "What is your secret to keep yourself looking so great?"

The conversation went something like this from that point. Mr. Boone replied, "Four things: First, I get plenty of rest."

Johnny Carson nodded, "I do that."

"Second, I exercise regularly."

"I do that, too."

"Third, I eat well and watch my diet."

Johnny nodded, "I do that."

"Fourth, I keep a clean conscience!"

Johnny bounced his pencil across the room, "You got me there!"

Good character shows! Is it showing in your life?

Summary:
Eleven Signs of Good Character

1. People of good character have self-confidence.
2. People of good character live within their means.
3. People of good character get along well with others.
4. People of good character have positively helpful attitudes.
5. People of good character have consideration of other people's needs.
6. People of good character have patience.
7. People of good character have a hunger for learning.
8. People of good character seek growth in skills and talent.
9. People of good character are reliable.
10. People of good character are unselfish.
11. People of good character are careful to love people and use things.

CHAPTER FIFTEEN

Learning to Feel and Express Gratitude

To have success on and off the job, you must develop an attitude of gratitude. If you cannot be grateful for what you have in possessions, relationships, and accomplishments, you will never be satisfied with anything the future may hold for you.

I know some people who don't seem to want to be satisfied. They always want to strive for bigger and better things. I understand that thinking, but if you feel no sense of accomplishment, if the more you do, the emptier you feel, you have a problem with a lack of gratitude. God has given us so much that if by comparison to others who have more, we degrade ourselves, as I have done, we miss out on some great blessings of life.

If you are ungrateful, people see it quickly, and they don't like to be around it. You may be told you're being fired for one thing, but it could be your ungrateful attitude that is at the heart of what lost the job. I hired a friend one time who should have been grateful to work in the same town in which he lived. It cut about an hour off his drive. His salary increased by about forty thousand dollars a year. Most who knew his situation considered him a very fortunate man.

However, the first day at work things became very sour. He was furious that he would not be rewarded with an office that had a window to the outside. It did not matter that others had been with the company for some years and were more deserving of an outside window. He just knew he wanted one, and he thought he couldn't live without it. His ungrateful attitude eventually led me to tell him he couldn't work there anymore. You see, the problem with the window was only the first of many issues where feelings were hurt over nothing of significance.

Let's take a look at your situation and determine if you need to do some work on developing an attitude of gratitude. If you will follow some of these suggestions, you may find your attitude changing and attitudes about you changing for the better. You may find people grateful that you are on board.

1. When was the last time you spoke to your boss for the sole purpose of expressing your gratitude for having a job? (There is nothing more wonderful to a boss than to hear those words.) If you are a boss, when was the last time you expressed your gratitude for your employees?

2. What is the one thing that you are the most grateful for on your job?

3. What would you miss most if you lost your job?

Learning to Feel and Express Gratitude

4. What is the one thing you could do today with a grateful attitude to ensure your job security?

5. Is there anyone who needs to know that you are changing your attitude? In other words, do you need to make a confession or two about past ungraciousness?

6. What is the number one threat to your attitude, and what can you do to counter it?

There are a lot of ways people block out gratitude from their lives and those around them. Their ungrateful thoughts are the ones that keep them constantly searching for something better. Here are a few comments they internalize to sap out the gratitude from the spirit:

- "If only . . ."
- "It's great, but . . ."
- "I'm so mad, I can't enjoy anything!"
- "You ruined it for me."
- "It would be perfect, except . . ."
- "Don't try to cheer me up."

These comments are typical of the negative attitudes that many people live with, and they hinder a grateful attitude. According to their way of thinking, there's always something, someone, or some other reason they can't really appreciate the good things in life.

We may refuse to be grateful because of these reasons:

1. In spite of what we do have, which may be quite a lot, there's that one important thing we don't have.

WINNING AT WORK

2. We feel major bitterness toward God or some person, and it ruins our appreciation of everything else.
3. Perfectionism keeps us from being delighted with anything.
4. We're afraid of happiness.
5. We feel cheated or victimized by life and refuse to celebrate.
6. Other people have more than we do.
7. We resent the timing—it would have been better if it had happened ten years ago.
8. We can't see the good in what little we have.
9. We want more.
10. We're afraid to enjoy it because we're afraid we'll lose it.

Developing an attitude of gratitude is well worth the effort. Seneca once said, "He who receives a benefit with gratitude repays the first installment on his debt."

A basic step you can take toward enjoyment of life's richest and fullest meaning is the development of a spirit of gratitude. You have so much to be grateful for. You have so many to be grateful to. You have a list of things to be grateful about. Yet you may feel unable to enjoy the pleasures of life.

Have you ever stopped to consider or catalogue the many things you have to be grateful for? It's a worthwhile exercise to actually write down everything you can think of, and to take a moment to thank God for what He's enabled you to have. Keith Green, the Christian evangelist and singer who died in 1982, used to teach people to pray with a grateful heart. His rule of thumb was to pray giving thanks for everything you have as if anything you failed to give thanks for would immediately disappear the moment you said, "Amen!" This kind of perspective will significantly influence those things for which you offer thanks.

Learning to Feel and Express Gratitude

Take the time to write down some of the great blessings that you possess today.

That old adage about counting your blessings is more than a positive-thinking technique. In Christianity, for example, there is a specific teaching that says, "In everything give thanks" (1 Thess. 5:18). Oddly enough, that doesn't just mean being thankful, or grateful, in the good times. It includes the bad times, too. "In everything"—the problems and the disappointments—we are to give thanks. Notice that it says *in* everything, not *for* everything. You are not expected to give thanks for something terrible, but in every situation you can find something for which to be grateful.

Does that sound unrealistic? It probably does unless you understand that the teaching is based on a belief in a good, loving God who has control of your life. Being grateful in bad things means reaching beyond your understanding with faith and saying, "It's going to work out for the good eventually. I just can't see it now."

Sometimes we are reluctant to give thanks. At those times we are to offer a sacrifice of thanksgiving. A sacrifice is often costly. The times when we don't see immediate reasons for thanksgiving are the times we may need to broaden our perspective to see what we really have for which we are truly grateful.

Our gratitude shouldn't stop with God. We have many people in our lives who deserve our thanks, and that list usually begins with our families. Of course, we know well the faults of family members, and it's sometimes easy to focus on the things we dislike the most.

How long has it been since you said, "Thanks—I love you!" to these people?

• Your parents
• Your brothers

WINNING AT WORK

- Your sisters
- Your grandparents
- Your spouse
- Your children
- Your aunts and uncles
- Your in-laws
- Your stepparents or stepchildren

Maybe you've got nothing to thank your family for, and if that's really the case, it's unfortunate. But so often, we take it for granted that people know how we feel—that we're grateful to them, love them, and value them. Particularly when dealing with older people, we sometimes wait too long, and by the time we're ready to speak up, it's too late.

Beyond families, our friends deserve our gratitude. And when we move out of the personal realm into the professional, we have a whole new list of reasons to say, "Thanks, you've been great."

Last year I received a Thanksgiving card that was somewhat unusual. This person makes a practice of giving thanks to her family and business associates at Thanksgiving time. Instead of waiting for Christmas to send out cards, she lists all the people she is grateful to and specific things for which she is grateful. Then she sends notes to the people to express her gratitude for specific ways her life was blessed by theirs. I think this is a great idea. Next Thanksgiving season, don't limit your celebration to giving thanks over a turkey dinner. Remember to give thanks to your friends and family for all they mean to you.

Learning to Feel and Express Gratitude

THE ART OF EXPRESSING GRATITUDE

If you want people to like being around you and be willing to be around you, use these six expressions of gratitude.

1. Express Gratitude Genuinely and Honestly

There is nothing worse than the feeling people get when they feel like they are being manipulated with insincere praise. Gratitude without substance is worse than no gratitude at all. If you are not pleased with a person's job, don't manipulate by saying something that is not true.

Often a person is doing something that doesn't meet with our approval, and we put off confronting it and resolving it. As we remain bothered over the inadequacy, we overlook many of the good things that the person is doing. The best approach for everyone is to confront the negative performance in as positive a way as possible, resolve the issue, and then get on with finding things to be grateful about in the job performance.

Be genuine and sincere as you look for excuses to express how grateful you are that this person has decided to dedicate time and talent to your operation.

2. Express Gratitude Specifically

Being specific in your expressions of gratitude is the only way you can be sure a person knows you are genuine and sincere. Don't just say, "It's nice to have you working with me." Be specific about a project or a task that deserves a word of praise. To do that you will have to be sure your formal and informal information network is in place; otherwise those specifics that need to be brought up will be passed by.

3. Express Gratitude Unreservedly

I worked for a man who at times would be impressed with the job that I had done. Considering the amount of bonus dollars I earned him, he should have been very grateful. It was hard for him to say he was grateful. I often think the reserve he showed stemmed from a fear that if he praised me too much, I might think I didn't need him and I would move on. I stuck with that guy for a lot of years before receiving an offer I couldn't turn down. I wonder how long I would have stayed if he had been a bit freer with his praise.

Be sure that if you do praise someone, you don't pull back the compliment as soon as you give it by saying something like the following:

- "You aren't nearly as limited in what you can do as I thought you were."
- "You are much better at this than you used to be."
- "That's not bad for someone in your position."

If you are going to praise people in a backhanded way, it might be better not to praise them at all.

4. Express Gratitude Frequently

One of the great benefits of expressing gratitude frequently is that you become a grateful person. It helps people you work with, and it helps you. It gives you the attitude of a winner. Winners seem to be able to find the good news in the midst of the bad and are grateful for it. To motivate people, you need to be the one who is always finding another way to express gratitude.

Making lists is a good way to find all the elements of a person's performance to express gratitude about. Evaluate by writing down what you think the person does extremely well. If you can't find a lot of things that are obvious, perhaps you

Learning to Feel and Express Gratitude

have a problem, or you have the wrong person working for you.

5. Express Gratitude Widely

People who work close to you will benefit from your being able to express specific and frequent gratitude. But people who work in remote locations or positions also need to hear your gratitude. Use faxes, company newsletters, and phone calls to let people know that you are grateful for their working with the company and that they are all partners with you on the mission you are trying to accomplish.

6. Express Gratitude Publicly

Most people like to be praised publicly. Have in place both formal and informal systems to reward those who are making an exceptional contribution to the organization. Give away plaques and certificates. Hand them out personally, and take pictures of the presentation event. Take care that these don't occur for outstanding performance only; include things like reliability, dependability, and longevity.

These six elements can be adequately expressed only when they come from a person with a truly grateful heart and attitude. You can learn to take the focus off yourself and turn your gratitude toward heaven. Develop a grateful attitude by regularly expressing thanks to God for both your talents and your opportunities. Don't wait for life to be perfect before you get around to being thankful. When you learn to feel and express gratitude, you will be able to appreciate the meaning of your life, making you a winner all the way around.

WINNING AT WORK

Summary:
The Art of Expressing Gratitude

1. Express gratitude genuinely and honestly.
2. Express gratitude specifically.
3. Express gratitude unreservedly.
4. Express gratitude frequently.
5. Express gratitude widely.
6. Express gratitude publicly.

CHAPTER SIXTEEN

Reflecting on a Whole and Fulfilling Life

Watching Darryl fall apart was like watching a building collapse in slow motion, from the inside out. It was tragic and unnecessary. Those of us who cared about him saw the danger, but we couldn't approach him with our warnings. He refused to hear us. And so we watched helplessly.

He was a highly successful professional, with a resume that could only intimidate those who sought to compete with him. His education had come from the finest learning institutions in the world, including Harvard and Oxford. He was good-looking and well spoken. He always seemed to be in the right place at the right time. His upward spiral in the business community was legendary, written up in major magazines as an example of how one gifted man can have it all.

Darryl's marriage wasn't happy. And despite all his professional expertise, he had no idea how to cope with his emotional bruises and failures. Characteristic of many men, he escaped into his career, and he created a pattern of workaholism that enabled him to almost forget his domestic woes. He traveled extensively, and when he was home, he stayed up late catching up on bills, mail, and other tasks that had been put on hold during his absence. He used trips as an escape, and he used the time away as an excuse for not confronting problems.

As the years went by, Darryl drove himself more and more relentlessly. His idea of taking care of his body was reflective of his inexhaustible energy—he ran an hour a day. He included church activities in his busy schedule, but he always assumed that the personal aspects of religion were for someone else—women, philosophers, or people with serious illnesses. Sure, he prayed when he was in a bind, but God was just as busy as he was and should be contacted only in emergencies.

Darryl kept his mind focused on a jumble of career responsibilities. He was usually in a mental frenzy about the many things he'd left undone because of his frantic pace. He became progressively disorganized and unbelievably forgetful. And instead of acknowledging these problems, he became defensive when he was late or unreliable. The more mistakes he made, the more arrogant he became. His attitude stated flatly, "A man in my position doesn't have to meet other people's expectations."

Darryl didn't allow anyone to get truly close to him. He was flattering to his friends but cold to them when they called him at the wrong time. The one exception was the various women with whom he became infatuated over the years. He toyed with them, slept with them, but resented their attempts to own him. Those romantic relationships were short-lived, and they always felt burdensome to him.

Ultimately, Darryl's health broke. As he moved into his fifties, his body could no longer support the hectic pace he

Reflecting on Life

required to avoid facing his deep personal problems. Cholesterol clogged his veins. Stress-related conditions slowed him down, and the need to slow down terrified him. Sadly, Darryl's story ended in sudden and early death. Darryl had not understood that life cannot be fulfilling on the whole if it is one-dimensional or out of balance.

THE THREE-LEGGED STOOL

The most stable seating available is a three-legged stool. Milkmaids throughout history could attest to this fact. The triangle at the base provides unparalleled stability. The illustration of the three-legged stool is helpful when we consider the three elements of successful living that contribute to a whole and fulfilling life. The three legs of the stool represent the three elements of life dealt with in this book: the mission, the money, and the meaning:

- If we focus too much on the meaningful side of life, we'll have no money, and we'll never accomplish the mission. We also might spend so much in bringing meaning to ourselves and others that we run out of money.
- If we focus too much on the mission, we'll lose sight of our financial responsibilities, and we'll forget to enjoy daily pleasures. Most likely we will leave our families far behind, and we will view them as nothing more than obligations or inconveniences.
- If we focus too much on money or never learn to acquire and manage money, we'll find ourselves selling out the mission and living in a world devoid of wonder and meaning. We'll become consumed by the money we make, and the vacuum of meaning will grow greater with each new day.

WINNING AT WORK

FINDING NEW BALANCE

A recent article from the Associated Press reports that one of the positive by-products of the raging unemployment in the United States has been a renewed spirituality. When people cease to define themselves by their jobs, they find their faith deepening. This typifies how the off-balance life can be set right when too much emphasis on one area is removed.

The same holds true for the man who is suddenly stricken by illness. He lies on his sickbed and evaluates his life's mission—where is he going, what is really important, and how many of his goals has he reached?

Of course, no one wants to be faced with a crisis in order to set priorities right, and an ounce of prevention is worth a pound of cure. Take a look at the following list of ten essential items to consider to ensure that you have balance in the emotional, physical, and spiritual areas of your life:

1. Your handwritten obituary (what you'd like said about yourself at your funeral). Focusing on how you want your life to conclude will cause your mind to focus on how to reach that conclusion at every turn.

2. A group of advisors who meet with you regularly and always tell you the truth. If you don't already meet with a small group, you can start your own or join a small group offered by a club, church, or support organization.

3. A close confidant(e) who cares more about you personally than about your career. It is wise to choose someone of the same sex if you're married or to make your spouse your confidant(e). Sharing your heart with another person often leads to other forms of intimacy.

4. A weekly class that will teach you something com-

pletely new. Community education classes are available in most areas. Take a class in art, a foreign language, cooking, or anything stimulating that will require no homework. Winston Churchill had a passion for oil painting throughout his adult life. He said the experience of using a different part of his brain seemed to make him better able to return to his work and family more focused.

5. A two-week family vacation. Don't neglect this! If possible, don't split the time. It may take one week just to unwind and get your business off your mind.

6. A commitment to manage the family's money as diligently as you manage your corporation's. If you are lacking in this area, don't put off dealing with family finances until you can do it all. Make a list of goals related to getting family finances in order. Take them one at a time. Work together with other family members, and applaud progress.

7. Your latest physical exam results—including cholesterol readings. Once you have an accurate reflection of your physical condition, you need to make a commitment to adjust your lifestyle to correct any problem areas.

8. Your plans to pass your position on to your successor, including the date of your resignation. This will keep you looking ahead and growing. It has been said that a rut is nothing more than a grave with the top and bottom extended. Stay alive by seeing that where you are today is not the end (even if you are retired). Set fresh goals continually.

9. A weekly lunch date with your spouse. During this time, don't talk business. Don't go over the day-to-day work of home or office. Use this time to hear how your spouse is feeling. Have a heart-to-heart conversation.

10. A fifteen-minute interlude every morning for contemplation and spiritual renewal. Call it quiet time, meditation, reflection, or prayer, a time of spiritual renewal is essential. M. Scott Peck, who wrote the best-seller *The Road Less Traveled,* began taking short times for prayer each day. He found that he benefited so much and was better able to keep his life in balance that he expanded the time from a few minutes to two hours each day.

These are the things that can ensure you are not avoiding the meaning of life at the expense of the mission and the money or focusing on any one element of life to the exclusion of others. Meaning comes when you take the time to reflect on what you want to accomplish other than accumulating money.

THE FIVE DIMENSIONS OF LIFE

Human existence can be seen in terms of five dimensions: (1) physical, (2) mental, (3) emotional, (4) social, and (5) spiritual. And despite his remarkable worldly success over the years, Darryl was negligent in every one of those five areas. He was tragically irresponsible. He was self-abusive. It cost him everything.

#1: Physical

Taking care of our bodies is more than a good idea. It is the first step toward any kind of success. Unfortunately, many men take better care of their cars than they do their bodies. And women aren't a lot better—they rush the children off to the pediatrician at the slightest sneeze and ignore their own major symptoms of disease.

Sometimes, we're afraid to go because of what we'll hear once the doctor really takes a close look. Other times, we're

Reflecting on Life

either too busy or too convinced "that could never happen to me" to be realistic about stress, aging, and other risks. Here are a few basic tips for better health:

- Make your physical health a primary priority in your life.
- Put yourself under the care of a doctor, and choose him or her carefully. If you're selective about accountants, public relations firms, and consultants, you should be equally careful in selecting your doctor.
- Have a baseline strength test and a cardiovascular measurement taken. You may be able to do this at a YMCA. Then use the information as a standard for what you need to improve and to track your progress.
- Inform yourself about cholesterol, and be sure you are up to date on your own levels including low-density lipoproteins (LDL) and high-density lipoproteins (HDL).
- Determine your resting heart rate. This is an indicator of your overall health.
- Have an annual examination whether you think you need to or not. Some diseases have no symptoms until they have progressed dangerously.
- Commit to a steady exercise program, and follow it religiously. Don't exchange working out for working, or your work may be cut short with your life.
- Pay attention to persistent physical symptoms and find out what is causing them. It's better to be safe than sorry.
- Eat regularly. Don't overeat, and don't skip meals.
- Get adequate amounts of sleep.
- Have a massage once in a while. It helps to reduce

stress. Besides it just feels great! Be kind to your-self when you need it.

- Don't believe the lie that you are indestructible.

#2: Mental

Our minds are valuable treasures. They may not always work the way we'd like them to, but we have a responsibility to keep them functioning properly. It's been said, "As a man thinketh, so is he," and in many ways this is true.

Our thought lives are the soil from which our actions sprout, grow, and bear fruit—for better or for worse. Rarely do we act without having daydreamed, fantasized, or calculated first. Jesus taught that even when our behavior appears to be righteous, we are unrighteous if the thoughts in our minds are evil. This, of course, presents a major problem to most of us. Cleaning up our thought lives isn't easy. In fact, it's impossible.

To make matters worse, when we're busy and burdened with responsibilities, we face a sort of mental gridlock. So many problems, ideas, challenges, fears, and possibilities are racing around our brains that they begin to back up, and we find ourselves immobilized on some overpass, unable to re-member what we're doing, where we're going, or what seemed so important thirty seconds ago. The name for this condition is stress. It affects our bodies and spirits, but it originates in our minds.

If you're facing mental gridlock, take a look at several things you can do to alleviate stress:

- Stop and change routine.
- Break out of an introspective mode.
- Get rid of grudges.
- Exercise.
- Choose to be happy.

- Think about positive things.
- Live in the now.
- Listen to music.
- Read positive materials.
- Get on your knees.

#3: Emotional

Even if we are strong mentally and healthy physically, we can sabotage ourselves emotionally. It is in the emotional area where our wounds disable us. And as those wounds eat away at our souls from the inside, we sometimes compound the problem by making foolish decisions to ease the pain. Unaware of what we're doing, we get involved in addictions or other unhealthy behaviors, and in doing so, we aggravate the wound. That was Darryl's problem, and he never solved it.

Finding emotional health is essential to permanent, well-balanced success. Yet we frequently prefer the head-in-the-sand approach to our emotions: if I don't think about them, they'll go away.

On the other hand, we may use our changeable and unreliable feelings as a compass. Feelings guide us in the wrong direction just as often as in the right one. They can't be trusted, yet they feel more important than anything else when we're in the midst of an emotional storm.

It's worth repeating: the healing of emotional wounds is a priority for all of us. We have to acknowledge our wounds, identify them, and work toward their eventual healing (see chapter 1). Once we're in the process of seeing those wounds healed, we still have to deal with the daily necessity of maintaining a good attitude—the kind of attitude that will fuel us, not fool us.

With the right attitude, we can accomplish more than we ever dreamed. With the wrong attitude, we will ignore more opportunities than most people ever get. Are you being the best you can be? Check yourself against this list of being the best you can be, and see how you measure up. Then work on your weak spots.

- Don't put limitations on yourself. What would you do if you knew you could not fail? You cannot control the outside—only what is inside your life.
- Make only choices that are good for you. You are the result of the choices you make. Don't make excuses for bad choices—take responsibility, admit your shortcomings, and move on toward your goal.
- Don't worry about what others think about you. No one can live your life but you. Do what is best and right for you regardless of what others might think.
- Determine to have a healthy body. Treat your body as if it is the only one you are going to get. Use positive self-talk to program staying well. Practice wellness.
- Take control of your life and responsibility for your feelings. Stop blaming others for the things that are wrong in your life. Take charge!
- Live every day to its fullest. How much more would you do if you approached every day as if it might be your last?

#4: Social

Every person alive needs friends. And when we surround ourselves with trusted friends, we benefit ourselves, and we give of ourselves to those we care about. But many of us have been burned in friendships that seemed safe and turned out to be treacherous.

Reflecting on Life

In the competitive professional world, we have to be "wise as serpents and gentle as doves" when it comes to our social lives. It's one thing to make small talk at a dinner party. "My secretary will call your secretary and we'll pencil a time to do lunch" isn't likely to have major repercussions in the future.

But making real friends is quite another story. As we get older, we treasure the friends who have seen us through the good times and the bad times, and we're more cautious about opening up to new people.

Here are several thought-provoking guidelines about safe people that might help you evaluate potential candidates for friendship:

- Safe people aren't afraid of intimacy.
- Safe people put a high price on honesty.
- Safe people are focused on reality, not fantasy.
- Safe people aren't needy and dependent.
- Safe people say, "I'm sorry."
- Safe people aren't put off by others' faults.
- Safe people are involved in their own personal growth.
- Safe people are reliable and responsible.
- Safe people know how both to give and to take constructive criticism, but they aren't critical.
- Safe people mirror to you your real self.
- Safe people give as comfortably as they take.
- Safe people remind you of your value and affirm you—without a hidden agenda.

A safe friend is an invaluable asset. I have one that I can tell everything, good and bad. He keeps me accountable and corrects some of my faulty thinking. If you don't have someone like that, you're missing out on a great winning ingredient.

WINNING AT WORK

#5: Spiritual

The spiritual side of life is often overlooked in our very material world. We are more likely to try to have more of what we can see, touch, and handle than to probe the mysterious depths of an unseen world. And yet that world is there.

A lot of people who go to church have taken the time to seek out truth about God and His plans and purposes for their lives. I happen to be a Christian believer, and my faith means a great deal to me. I feel that any success I have had, I stumbled onto it with the direction of God.

If you haven't addressed this area of your life, you are living in a spiritual void that accounts for much of the emptiness you feel. Whatever the reason you have abandoned your faith, take a second look. There are too many brilliant winners who have grand faith to overlook this as a valid part of anyone's life.

Many successful people make the horrible mistake of achieving success and then not having a means to enjoy it. A relationship with God is the number one guarantee that once you make it into the winner's circle, you will enjoy being there.

Here are some steps to help you grow spiritually:

- You must trust God more and money less. Use your money to help your family and others, but don't allow it to be your source of security. Work hard on your attitudes toward money. Ask God to move your heart away from dependence on money and more toward dependence on Him.
- You must allow God to heal your wounds. He must heal you before you further wound yourself, before you wound people you love. God will do this for you. God cares enough to reach out from eternity to meet your specific and unique needs.

Reflecting on Life

Jeremiah 6:14 says that you can't heal a wound by saying it's not there. Admit that you have wounds, and then bring them before God to be healed. He will turn your wounds into your greatest strengths.

- You must guard your heart. You do this by sticking close to your faith and your family and avoiding the temptations of the world. Deny yourself worldly pleasures that begin with lust and greed. Establish a lifestyle that prevents you from falling into sin that will ruin you and your family. Make a decision away from promiscuity and toward integrity.

REFLECTING ON YOUR LIFE

Many hardworking people do not take the time for personal evaluation. They avoid introspection. And they rarely allow themselves the appreciation of beauty and spiritual aspects of life. Reflection and contemplation are integral to emotional, spiritual, and physical health. Many who have succeeded in enjoying whole and fulfilling lives credit their times of reflection with propelling their success. Thus, reflection times are good for the soul, and they also allow us to uncover some ideas and concepts and strengths that go unnoticed if we don't force ourselves to schedule in time to reflect. There are five essential abilities necessary for reflection.

1. The Ability to Quiet the Mind and Be Still Before God

At some point you have to stop figuring things out and listen to the still, small voice within. A proverb offers this insight:

Trust in the LORD with all your heart,
    And lean not on your own understanding;
    In all your ways acknowledge Him,
    And He shall direct your paths (Prov. 3:5–6).

WINNING AT WORK

Whether you are a cerebral person who likes to analyze circumstances or a doer who likes to take hold of life and make things happen, it isn't easy to stop, look, listen, and "trust in the LORD." To do so takes faith, discipline, and determination. And you can be sure—this sort of enforced silence is not a waste of valuable time!

François Fénelon commented on this idea by saying, "How can you expect God to speak in that gentle and inward voice which melts the soul, when you are making so much noise with your rapid reflections? Be silent and God will speak again."

Perhaps one reason people don't take time to be silent before God is that they are afraid He may speak and they are not prepared to listen!

2. The Ability to See and Hear the Lasting Qualities of the World Around You

One of the biggest killers in our present world is stress. And one of the reasons we are so infected by stress is that we lose sight of the really valuable and precious things that surround us every day. "Stop and smell the roses" is a cliché, but it has validity. It really means that there is a great danger in overlooking the best, the most lasting things life offers and focusing on nonessentials.

And speaking of nonessentials, one of the primary factors in stress, and one of the main reasons we don't enjoy life, can be summed up in one word: *worry*.

In Jesus' most well-known teaching, which is called the Sermon on the Mount, He gave these reasons for not worrying:

• Worry is illogical. It's a waste of time to worry about something you can't change. It's utter foolishness to worry about something you *can* change. And worry takes on a life of its own—it grows

Reflecting on Life

larger every time you exercise it and blows small things completely out of proportion. Jesus said, "Do not worry about your life, what you will eat or what you will drink; nor about your body, what you will put on. Is not life more than food and the body more than clothing?" (Matt. 6:25).

• Worry is unnatural. You had to learn to be a worrier. It didn't come to you as part of your personality. As far as we know, animals don't worry. In their simplicity, they seem to instinctively know that God is watching over them. Jesus said, "Look at the birds of the air, for they neither sow nor reap nor gather into barns; yet your heavenly Father feeds them. Are you not of more value than they?" (Matt. 6:26).

• Worry is useless. It accomplishes nothing. It can't reinvent your past. It can't affect your future. All it does is ruin your day, along with your ability to savor your present blessings. Jesus said, "Which of you by worrying can add one cubit to his stature?" (Matt. 6:27).

• Worry is worthless. If you have faith, you have all you need to take care of you. You will be shown what to do and what not to do. You will be given the things you need, and you have been told to entrust God with the details of your life. Jesus said, "Therefore do not worry, saying, 'What shall we eat?' or 'What shall we drink?' or 'What shall we wear?' . . . For your heavenly Father knows that you need all these things" (Matt. 6:31–32).

• Worry robs you of present pleasure. You are always borrowing troubles from the future when you worry. Jesus said, "Do not worry about tomorrow, for tomorrow will worry about its own

things. Sufficient for the day is its own trouble"
(Matt. 6:34).

Once you've come to see the futility of your worry habit,
you'll be better able to clear your mind of anxious thoughts
and really enjoy the scenery, the company you're with, the
good food you're eating, the weather, the garden, or simply
the peace and quiet of a few moments alone.

3. The Ability to Grasp the Deeper Meaning of Life

Our materialistic culture has a "seeing is believing" philosophy. We tend to think that if we can't grasp and categorize something in our minds, it doesn't exist. Faith in God,
however, requires us to believe what we cannot see. True faith
claims to be the substance and the evidence of the unseen.
There are times when we have to look beyond the surface to
see the deeper meaning of life.

Sometimes grasping the deeper meaning of life involves
facing up to something we need to know or do. A thoughtful
look at life may mark the end of our denial about some unpleasant truth. And ending denial is bound to bring to life
some wonderful new beginnings.

Therapists agree that more than a third of us want to
make a major change in our lives. An even larger number have
wanted to make that change for more than five years. If your
head is filled with those little self-admonishing voices saying
things like, "I really should lose weight," or "I know I need to
get in shape," or "Someday I am going to have to do something about my temper," or whatever you tell yourself you
need to change, it takes more than thinking about it. You have
to take a deeper look at your life. You have to take a first step
in a new direction.

If you're ready to take a deeper look, here are some
thoughts about change and the steps you need to make to

231

R e f l e c t i n g   o n   L i f e

initiate it. Change may have to do with your job, your relationships, your personal habits, or other circumstances.

Step #1: Stop lying to yourself.

Step #2: Take a hard look at what's troubling you. Inform yourself about the facts.

Step #3: Readjust your priorities. Don't allow yourself to be impulsive, and take enough time to carefully prepare for a new beginning.

Step #4: Surround yourself with supportive friends who will tell you the truth.

Step #5: Seek guidance, help, and courage from God.

Step #6: Just do it!

Even when your circumstances aren't in need of change, you are still capable of "not seeing the forest for the trees." You need to understand that there is more to life than the superficial activities that fill your hours. As you begin to grasp this, you will deepen the quality of your life and leave behind you a trail of significant contributions that have true spiritual value.

4. The Ability to See People as Individuals

Every person you know has hopes, dreams, strengths, and weaknesses. The men and women who populate houses, offices, neighborhoods, clubs, and other surroundings are not simply objects. They have not been placed in your path as implements to help you meet your goals, fulfill your mission, or provide for your needs. Do you really believe that? You ought to ask yourself a pertinent question and demand an honest answer:

Am I a giver
or
a taker?

Not only do you need to ask this question in general. You need to ask it in terms of how you relate to each person in your life. You may be primarily a giver in one relationship or setting and a taker in another. You must also consider the question in terms of degrees. Levels of giving and taking differ in propriety, depending on the nature of the relationship, and change with time.

The way you treat your family and friends is going to reflect the value you place on each person as an individual who is uniquely designed and of infinite value. You may be so interested in what they can give you that you fail to realize how much they need from you. The irony is, the more you give to them, the more they will be able to return to you in helping you achieve your goals. If you take enough, there will eventually be nothing left to take.

You must also guard against taking too much from people who work with you. When you are dealing with people professionally, you do yourself an immense favor when you treat them with respect and value. Rabbi Harold Kushner cites some principles to remember when dealing with business associates:

- Keep relationships humane. Compassionate, caring relationships in the marketplace are not only ethically right; they are good for business.
- Don't overidentify with the company. The company's success doesn't mean that you're a genius,

and its difficulties don't mean that you're a loser.
As it's put in Ecclesiastes in the Bible, "The race is
not always to the swift nor the battle to the strong,
for time and chance enter into all things."

• Life is about people, not profits. Realize that your
immortality will ultimately come not from business success but from your relationships.

If you want to consider whether you are being balanced
and fair in your business dealings, ask yourself the following
questions. It would be better if you could get candid answers
from people you work with. However, chances are that they
would not risk damaging the balance of power if the answers
were not what you want to hear. When considering the fairness of your business dealings, ask yourself,

• If I was being asked to perform as I expect others
to perform, would I find that acceptable?
• If I was being offered the deal I offer a business
associate, would I accept the terms? If not, why
would I expect another to?
• Do I justify expecting performance of others I
would not find acceptable or making an offer to
someone I would not agree to myself because I see
myself as better than the other person?
• Do I ever take advantage of others because I know
their resources and options are limited?

5. The Ability to Know Yourself

When reflecting on your whole life, you must consider
not only the parts of your life but also the *way you view and
think about* the parts of your life. Some people view life as
what I call reactive thinkers. They tend to react to and against
what happens to them. Others are creative in the way they

view and think about their lives. They are what I call creative thinkers. The creative thinker does not simply react. The creative thinker learns to look at the whole of life and creatively mix all the elements in a way that brings fulfillment. You can learn to be a creative thinker.

Much of what I suggest in these pages will call out your creativity, calling you to do more with your life than just react day to day. Following are some of the characteristics demonstrated by these differing perspectives from which to reflect on your life. Consider the ways in which you may display the characteristics of each perspective.

Reactive thinkers

- are resistant to change.
- see reasons they cannot do things.
- focus on finding problems to fix.
- are blinded by problems in a situation.
- avoid blame or responsibility.
- are limited by what worked in the past.
- are poor listeners.
- run out of energy quickly.
- find it difficult to choose and decide.
- feel they have no control of their environment.
- often work very hard.
- are afraid of risks or major challenges.
- suffer excessive inner stress.
- cannot let go of the past.
- are devastated by failure.
- have low self-esteem.
- focus on what they want to avoid.
- do things right.

Creative thinkers

- are open to change.
- are "can-do" oriented.

Reflecting on Life

- build on successes and strengths.
- seek the opportunity in situations.
- take responsibility for their actions.
- think in terms of new possibilities.
- are good listeners.
- have a continuous supply of energy.
- make choices and decisions easily.
- feel in control of their environment.
- get results without trying hard.
- are driven to excel by challenge or risk.
- enjoy an inner calmness.
- are current and future oriented.
- learn and grow from their mistakes.
- have high self-esteem.
- focus on results they want.
- do the right things.

Before you can help yourself, you need to know yourself. To truly know yourself, you must take time to reflect and evaluate. Some of the best parts of who you are will come out only when you carefully reflect on who you are, where you are, and what God can do when you put your best talents to work. This puts meaning into life and into your work. I hope this book becomes a tool you will use to reflect on what it means to have a whole and fulfilling life. Then you will be able to take the steps necessary to experience winning at work without losing at love.

Summary:
Five Essential Abilities for Reflection

1. Quiet the mind and be still before God.
2. See and hear the lasting qualities of the world around you.
3. Grasp the deeper meaning of life.
4. See people as individuals.
5. Know yourself.

About the Author

Stephen Arterburn is the cofounder and chairman of Minirth Meier New Life (MMNL) Clinics, which has more than fifty clinics in operation across the nation. He is currently the cohost of the MMNL radio program with a listening audience of over one million. He is a nationally known speaker and has made regular appearances on television talk shows such as "Oprah," "Sally Jessy Raphael," "Geraldo," and "Inside Edition." He is the author of seventeen books, including *Gentle Eating, The Angry Man, Addicted to "Love,"* and *Faith that Hurts, Faith that Heals.* Arterburn holds degrees from Baylor University and the University of North Texas and has been awarded two honorary doctorate degrees. In 1993 he was named Socially Responsible Entrepreneur of the Year by *Inc. Magazine,* Ernst and Young, and Merrill Lynch. Arterburn and his wife, Sandy, and daughter, Madeline, live in Laguna Beach, California.

If you are interested in having Stephen Arterburn speak to your organization or at a special event, please contact:

> **interAct Speaker's Bureau**
> 330 Franklin Road
> Suite 120, Box 897
> Brentwood, TN 37024-8097
>
> 800-370-9932
> 615-370-9939 FAX

For assistance with a personal or emotional problem, call the Minirth Meier New Life Clinics at 1-800-NEW-LIFE.